RESILIENCE

RISING ABOVE
LIFE'S CHALLENGES

LISA MILLIKEN

innovo
PUBLISHING
innovopublishing.com

Published by Innovo Publishing, LLC
www.innovopublishing.com
1-888-546-2111

innovo
PUBLISHING
innovopublishing.com

Publishing quality books, eBooks, audiobooks, music, screenplays & courses for the Christian & wholesome markets since 2008.

RESILIENCE
Rising Above Life's Challenges

Library of Congress Control Number: 2024914878
ISBN: 979-8-88928-032-3

Cover Design & Interior Layout: Innovo Publishing, LLC

Printed in the United States of America
U.S. Printing History
First Edition: 2024

Has God called you to create a Christ-centered or wholesome book, eBook, audiobook, music album, screenplay, or online course? Visit Innovo's educational center (cpportal.com) to learn how to accomplish your calling with excellence.

To my amazing children, Alex Laycie & Jake, who constantly inspire me and remind me of what is most important.

Contents

Chapter 1

INTRODUCTION

Y OU KNOW THAT FEELING WHEN SOMETHING REALLY BAD IS ABOUT
to happen, and you struggle to figure out how you will survive
the blow? Or the sinking feeling of panic, agitation, and being
overwhelmed by outside circumstances after a horrible thing has just
happened? You may even be thinking, *How will I survive?* And if you
are like me and many other people, because we're human, you may
ask yourself, *Why did this happen? How could this even be possible?* And
finally, you succumb to wondering, *How can I move forward?* and in
what feels to be a blind, questioning moment with no solution in
sight, you wonder, *What is going to happen next?* and, *Will things ever
be normal again?*

In the subsequent moments, we may feel like we are all alone
and experiencing this big obstacle to life while everyone around us
seems to be living their normal, happy life. But that is not the case.
Though their social media accounts may show they are all happy,
celebrating life with perfect families and friends and showing no
signs of life challenges, they too have similar circumstances—either
past, present, or in the very near future.

I teach for a lot of conferences with a range of adult audiences, from church groups to professional health care participants. When I have asked the question, "Is there anyone here over the age of thirty who has not yet experienced a major life challenge or overwhelming adversity?"—in most cases, the room is silent. No hands go up. But on one occasion, a man in his mid-thirties sitting in the front row raised his hand. I responded, "Wow! That's great—and rare! So you've never had a major challenge or hurdle in life?" He responded, "No, I've had many of those already, but I just wanted to share that I *was* the major hurdle and challenge that my wife had to experience before I started to get my life together. And it was very difficult. But we're good now." His wife was sitting beside him, and they had apparently gotten through years of tough times together.

In addition to teaching, I find myself having long, personal conversations with friends and colleagues across the country. I should point out two things about myself here. First, I am an active listener. I look at people when they talk, nodding my head in understanding and trying not to interrupt. This seems to trigger the outpouring of things they need to say. The second thing is that I think of myself as a *HIPAA friend.* Since I've worked in health care for the past thirty-five-plus years, I learned long ago what true confidentiality means. So whatever people tell me, I hold that information securely in my mind and never disclose their secrets. The only exception is if they tell me they've abused a child, an elder, or a person with a disability. Then I would have to report such abuse to the authorities. Otherwise, I'm a safe, trusting friend. I've learned that people need that. We all need that.

Following such conversations, I realize no one has the perfect life. We're all in this together, though in different circumstances and in different struggles and battles. I can't recall a single conversation over the past few years where I left thinking that person has the perfect life with no struggles. Yet the thing that seems to be the most interesting to me is that I see we all respond to the circumstances differently. Some struggle to take even a single step forward. Others may have experienced the most unimaginable sequence of events and are positive and rising to new heights despite their circumstances. They appear resilient.

When reviewing the research of life stresses that require resilience, I saw this list of what they referred to as major life stressful events:

1. death of a loved one
2. divorce
3. financial issues
4. illness
5. job loss
6. medical emergencies
7. natural disasters

Such examples of extreme stress and challenges caught my attention because I have experienced each of the things on that list in addition to others. And I am not alone, as most people also have such life stresses along their journey. It is a part of life.

As already mentioned, I have many friends and colleagues who have experienced much more than me. It's interesting how some rise above so many more hardships and others crumble following fewer levels of stress points. But they may respond completely differently. The person who is able to handle challenges better than others is more resilient. In other words, they have a greater level of resiliency. In my case, I was able to handle some life stresses and situations better than others, but it often required every internal and external resource I could muster. In subsequent chapters of this book, I'll share examples of challenges in my own life. But I've also learned a great deal from others who experienced these challenges to a much greater extent and somehow survived and moved forward to great things. I explore how different people responded to different types of adversity. Many were and are the most positive people, who do not dwell on what they do not have. Instead, they focus on what they do have. Instead of spiraling into downward despair or hiding from issues by using unhealthy coping strategies, I have watched these resilient people directly face life's difficulties and move on to amazing successes. They are some of the most positive people I know.

It is also fascinating to study the scientific literature about how our brains and bodies respond differently to major stress. The facts show that people with resilience do not experience less distress, grief, or anxiety than other people do. They definitely experience the same stress and resulting pain—mental and physical signs of such stress. They are not immune to the deep emotions of grief, anxiety, and feelings of being overwhelmed. However, they practice resiliency-building strategies and utilize healthy coping skills to handle such difficulties in ways that foster strength and growth, often emerging stronger than they were before. I'll later share the strategies and characteristics for developing the highest level of resilience. But it is important to know, while some seem to have the innate ability to be resilient, everyone can still develop such abilities.

> **The facts show that people with resilience do not experience less distress. . . . However, they practice resiliency-building strategies and utilize healthy coping skills to handle such difficulties in ways that foster strength and growth, often emerging stronger than they were before.**

For the moment, let's consider this scenario: Think about how you would describe your response to a crushing event in your life. What was your response to the devastating loss of your dearest loved one? Or to another crisis you've faced? Reflecting on my initial responses to major blows in my life, I was often filled with high levels of anxiety, sometimes in the form of a full panic attack, as if I were falling off a cliff and couldn't pull myself back together to get on my feet again. But then, eventually two things happened:

1. I realized I *could* handle it, though it would be one step at a time, and I did have supportive friends who would be there along the way to get me through it.

2. I learned with wisdom from prior years of other related challenges that my strength is in my faith in God. He has gotten me through tougher times, and I survived. I will survive this as well, no matter how impossible and earth-shattering it seems to be at this moment.

If you have ever struggled to figure out how you will survive the blow, or if you are anywhere in the process of a challenge, know that resilience is possible. Within the following pages I will share with you strategies to build the strength you need, including examples from others who developed the resilience they needed through their trials. Oftentimes we are better and stronger after enduring the fight.

"We also glory in tribulations, knowing that tribulation produces perseverance; and perseverance, character; and character, hope. Now hope does not disappoint, because the love of God has been poured out in our hearts by the Holy Spirit who was given to us."

—Romans 5:3-5

Chapter 2

NO ONE IS IMMUNE TO LIFE STRESSES

I TRAVEL A LOT TO WORK WITH NURSING HOMES ON DIFFERENT projects and to teach conferences to new audiences. So I often get to meet many people across the country and hear their stories. I've also had long conversations with many patients over the last thirty-five years. It's interesting to note that while some people have overwhelming and tragic experiences that seem impossible to face, they are sometimes able to remain positive and encouraging, living their best possible life despite their circumstances. Others have less traumatic experiences but are still overwhelmed even years after their stressful events and have been unable to move on with life. In fact, they often seem to have worsened and struggle to function every day. Let me first share a few positive examples of people that I have met or stories that I've heard from close friends.

LARRY

A few years ago, I was gathering information to teach about the significant effects of music on people living with different disease processes, such as dementia, Parkinson's, and other neurodegenerative diseases. I had gathered all the research on the topic but wanted to see and hear real examples of what was working. As a part of this project, I visited a retirement community that included a memory care unit, a skilled nursing home, and other levels of care such as assisted living and independent living. I would have the opportunity to meet a variety of people throughout my visit. This happened to be a beautiful campus with state-of-the-art facilities and an excellent staff. The activity director was very helpful and got me set up to start with a review of the activity and music-related daily notes of residents that I would meet, to study the before-and-after clinical effects of music to their well-being outcomes.

I particularly enjoyed reading about this one man, as the notes stated that he was always very cheerful and brought joy to everyone's day. Let's just call him *Larry*. I read how he sang along with the music, told jokes, and seemed to be the life of the facility. I did not read any details about his clinical condition or diagnosis, as that was not my purpose. In health care we have strict confidentiality guidelines where only the health care provider working directly with a resident or patient should have access to a person's full medical records.

Next I went on rounds with the activity director, and she introduced me to different people, some of whom were wearing headphones with their favorite music being played. Finally we came to Larry's room, and I was anxious to get to meet him. My activity director guide asked him if she could tell me a little about his story, and he gave her permission to do so. She shared the story while interjecting a few additional facts along the way. It was the opposite of what I expected to hear about this joyful man. I also quickly recognized that he was paralyzed from the neck down.

Larry was a young pilot in the war, and his plane was shot down in Vietnam. Fortunately his body was recovered, but he was unconscious and could not move his extremities. Soldiers and medics on the ground had to quickly provide aid to those who were alive and move everyone out as fast as possible. In their haste, they assumed Larry was dead, so they put him in a body bag that was eventually put on a plane with other corpses in body bags to fly them back to the states. Larry recalled waking up while in that dark body bag on the long flight. He shared that he still remembers the smell of death all around him in that plane. He had no idea where he was or where he was going. He knew he could not move his hands or legs. He also wondered if he was dying or if he would survive whatever this was. He was terrified.

The story continued until they got to the present moment, where he is still alive in his mid-seventies and is living in a nursing home. He can only move his head and neck and requires complete care from staff for everything. But he chooses to be grateful for life and for the opportunity to be able to talk and use his brain. He very much enjoys music and conversations with friends or anyone who may stop by his room.

I'll never forget Larry. He chose to focus on what he still had rather than dwell on all that he had been through and all that he lost and never recovered. I'm sure he went through a lot in those weeks and months following his plane crash. He was not immune to the pain and every type of horrible thing he experienced. He could have chosen to stay in that mindset, dwelling on the thought that life was not fair. He could have resolved to be angry for the rest of his life. But Larry was resilient. In all his anguish and loss, he determined that he was going to make the very best of what he had. He would rise above the challenge and make a difference in other people's lives by bringing joy and cheerfulness to their day.

PATTY

One of my roommates following graduate school became my dear friend, Patty Mower. She is super fun with a quick wit. She has always been a very talented singer, so she received her music degree from

Jackson College of Ministries. Over the next thirty-nine years, she had many unique and interesting jobs, including serving as a music director for a church and their school (preschool through twelfth grade) in the San Francisco area, working for Tupelo Children's Mansion (a residential children's home), working for LeBonheur Children's Hospital, serving as a dispatcher/911 operator for the Memphis Police Department, and working for twelve years at a private nonprofit international adoption agency. She did a fair bit of travel for the adoption agency, with multiple trips to Romania and India, to identify and video *new* children available for adoption and/or to escort babies and toddlers to their forever homes. She stated, "I count the privilege of physically placing a child into their new parents' arms as high among the most meaningful and fulfilling things I've ever done." Then she worked at a law firm for fourteen years, supporting multiple attorneys with training programs, slide decks, documents, etc.

We sang together with our church praise team and spent much of our time together with a great group of early-career church friends. Patty has always been the one to say that one hilarious, dry-humor phrase that would make the entire room laugh. After several years of those fun days, I moved to Texas and lost touch with her. But thanks to social media, we found each other on Facebook and were able to get in touch again. Patty traveled to amazing places, got married to a great guy, continued her career with all her amazing jobs, and now lives in a great house in a great Memphis suburb.

Patty has dealt with spinal issues for years. I remember when we were roommates, one day she was walking through the living room, and when she took a normal step, her back went out. We had to get her to the couch, as she was completely unable to walk for the next few days. Back pain became a part of her life. Then finally, when she was fifty-three years old, she had fusion surgery, followed by another spinal surgery five years later. This resulted in her fused vertebrae from L-3 through S-1. However, her back and leg pain persisted.

Seven years following the first surgery, she was diagnosed with *failed back syndrome*, which is a chronic pain condition after spinal surgery. She was fitted with a trial external neurostimulator and describes the result as being nothing short of miraculous. For one week she had a pain reduction of about 80–90 percent and was able to walk and stand to her heart's content. Due to this success, they scheduled a permanent stim implantation. Seven days following the surgery, she went to the surgeon's office to get her staples removed, and he commented on how well she was healing. Patty and her husband would finally be able to go on their planned week of vacation to Destin, FL. The doctor cautioned her not to go in the water, but otherwise things should be fine.

The night before they would leave to drive to Florida, Patty started to feel bad with aches and a low-grade fever. But she finished packing and went to bed early, determined not to ruin their vacation. She was mostly thinking how she wanted this for her amazing husband, as they had waited so long to go on a real vacation. The next morning, she still wasn't feeling great, but they loaded the car and were on their way. By the time they got to Birmingham, about three and a half hours away, she was feeling much worse, and her incision began to seep and then pour. She told her husband, Steve, that she couldn't go any further, so they stopped at a hotel shortly thereafter. They called the weekend number for her physician and told them what was happening. The answering service called her surgeon, who said they needed to come back, and she needed to go to Methodist University ER. She couldn't travel any more that day, so the following morning, Sunday, they headed back.

Patty went to the ER on Monday and was taken into surgery. They found a MRSA infection inside the spinal column behind the vertebrae. They did one *washout* surgery and admitted her. The doctor told her she had "a ball of pus resting at the base of [her] spinal column." He performed another washout surgery, but by that time the damage was done. Patty had horrible, electric pain in her core area and shooting down both legs.

She went home with a PICC line and had daily antibiotic infusions for six weeks. Over time the severe electric *shock* sensations subsided, leaving her with severe neuropathy, resulting in very poor balance. She's fallen too many times to remember, despite the use of a walker. Due to her very unsteady gait on good days and inability to walk on other days, she is very fearful of leaving her home. Her biggest fear is falling somewhere away from home, which could result in a broken hip, ankle, or worse.

"My situation feels so precarious," Patty said. "To be honest, I was lost for a time. I was in survivor mode and was consumed with pain, both physical and mental. Overnight, my situation had drastically changed. I went from being able to walk (albeit with pain, but not needing a cane or walker) to being almost an invalid. It was a terrible time."

After about a year of this debilitating situation, she knew she had to figure out something to accomplish or achieve in her life. Something, anything, to get her beyond her four walls, even if it was figuratively beyond them. She found a therapist to help her come to terms with this new reality and to help her find joy in her life.

Patty had always enjoyed writing, mostly journaling. But she started writing much more. She found an international writing group and fell in love with it. This led to writing short stories, then poetry; then recently she completed a novel, which is in editing steps at this point. She has further planned for another novel and for a collection of her short stories. She recently shared, "Writing, and all the Zoom classes and writing sessions, has been a balm to my soul. Through all the friendships I've made with people around the world, I've gained a window to the world. It's absolutely been my saving grace. No exaggeration here."

Patty's newfound joy does not negate the pain or struggles. She still struggles with depression and fear of missing out (FOMO) when she sees how others can live and move and go and do. She struggles with guilt over denying her husband a fun retirement. They had planned many travels, but traveling is now too hard and painful for her. So it's still all a lot for her to deal with. But she's learned strategies to ground herself, to look beyond herself, and to find joy. She said, "My writing brings joy like nothing else these days."

PEYTON

Peyton is a beautiful young mom with an amazing husband and three young sons. She is devoted to her family as her top priority and has also been successful in her career as a speech language pathologist and aural rehabilitation specialist. She has worked in the public schools and currently serves as the assistant director of speech therapy services at Texas Hearing Institute in Houston, Texas. But if you only see this beautiful family on Facebook, you may never imagine their different levels of adversity over the last several years. She shares her story to maybe help others but also to help her grow in her own resilience.

As a young mother of a four-month-old infant, Peyton's husband was deployed, requiring new levels of strength and perseverance. Years later, when she was expecting her second child, she had a primary Cytomegalovirus (CMV) infection, which resulted in her own adverse effects. Fortunately her son was born without the virus. She recounts how supportive and amazing her husband has always been and how strong and amazing he is for her and her family, no matter the circumstances and challenges.

Her third child was born at thirty-five weeks after having a dangerously low heartbeat. He survived and spent two weeks in the NICU. During this stressful time, her oldest son told a daycare worker his dad hit him. Peyton's husband was at the hospital during this time, so the child's story was of course not true. But this story triggered an extensive Child Protective Services (CPS) investigation while they were in the hospital, praying for their son to survive.

When they were finally able to return home amid all they were going through, Peyton passed out in the shower. They later learned she had a uterine infection, requiring another seven days in the hospital. I can only imagine all the other details of the living nightmares they endured through their early years of marriage. But their faith was strong.

> **"Sharing our story kept the shame away. So that I could be resilient instead of full of shame, guilt, hurt. So many miracles. Only God could have made a way through it all."**

Peyton and her husband were there for each other to get through it all. She recalls how much she hated being in a situation where she needed or would have to ask for help. But she had no choice.

Families rallied together to care for their children. Her cousin stayed every night with her at the hospital. Their church family prayed. Their pastor visited them. Their friends offered to be references to CPS for them. So much prayer!

Peyton then shared, "I made our whole story public . . . the writing and the shared experiences of others help carry me through. I think sharing our story kept the shame away. So that I could be resilient instead of full of shame, guilt, hurt. So many miracles. Only God could have made a way through it all."

PAM

Pam is a successful woman who has recently retired from serving in multiple roles of academic and university leadership and is currently continuing as an adjunct faculty. Through her life, she has met and conquered many challenges in her rise to success. But several years ago, she experienced the most painful stress point of all when her brother died suddenly and unexpectedly in December of 2018, and then her mother died nine days later, two days after Christmas. These were the two closest family members to her, so the sudden loss of both was almost unbearable.

She then shared that she has over twenty years of sobriety. She stated, "If you want to ask me what resilience is, it's staying sober through something like that." She was listed as the administrator of her brother's estate, and he died without a will, so this was another big challenge that further tested her resilience.

Since Pam is experienced and knowledgeable in seeking research and evidence-based science to determine the needed solutions, she conducted literature searches to learn about why and how her family members had died. In gathering the facts to study, she learned that her brother was a hoarder, so she further researched this and learned a lot about her early family experiences and how they affected her family members differently.

When asked about her strategies for resilience, she shared that she initially used walking and exercise to help her through the difficulties. But now she has been diagnosed with severe osteoarthritis and has an upcoming orthopedic surgery consult. This brings a new question and challenge regarding not knowing what will happen next. But she seeks further resilience to get through the next levels of challenges.

Pam has also resorted to compartmentalization, which includes throwing herself into other productive things, though she recognizes the degree of approach-avoidance with that technique. She searches for productive things that she *can* do, such as teaching, doing yoga, and spending time with her husband and friends. Pam lives each day focusing on what she can control, adopting and maintaining healthy habits, cultivating supportive relationships, and practicing gratitude. One day at a time with these healthy habits is important.

SUSAN

I frequently meet and get to know people at my weekend conferences. We have one-on-one conversations, and I learn a lot about them over a few days' time. I met one lady who was an occupational therapist. Let's call her Susan. She's successful, has a wonderful husband and children, and lives in a great home and neighborhood. But eight months ago, she lost her brother to a progressive disease process. He was only sixty years young. She was very close to her dear brother, and grief has been harder for her than she thought. She's still in the anger stage of the grieving process and only wants to tell everyone she meets that life is not fair and she doesn't know why he had to die. It's the only topic she can talk about.

She asked me how I can work in nursing homes and with older people for most of my life, knowing that they may die at any point. I shared that I have felt the deep loss of many patients through the years. I've become very close to the people I saw for therapy and then continued to be their friend, stopping and checking on them and saying hello. So when I would get the news that they went to the hospital and passed away, I would sometimes have to clock out and go sit in my car and cry for an hour or more before I could pull myself together to go back to work. So yes, it is very hard for any of us to lose the people for whom we learned to care about so much.

I told Susan that I love what I do because I choose to focus on all the ways I've been able to help my patients. I got them off the PEG tube so they could eat their favorite foods again. I taught them how to talk or communicate their important thoughts again. I helped them to sing their favorite songs when they may struggle to talk. I played a role, along with my fellow physical and occupational therapists, to help people recover from strokes and other major illnesses and be able to go home again. In other words, I choose to focus on all the good things about our jobs and how we help people. I don't focus on the fact that they will one day pass away. We have the opportunity to bring joy and quality of life to people while they are still here.

I encouraged Susan to make herself think of all the things for which she is grateful. At any given point, we can all come up with a list of what we are worried about, what makes us sad, or how life is not fair. No one is immune to those things. However, we can also come up with an even longer list of what we have to be grateful for. Start with our own health. Think about having a place to live and food to eat. Most of us are able to take a hot shower every day. Many of us have the ability to walk and talk and spend time with friends or loved ones. I am not saying that Susan should not grieve. Grief is inevitable. It's a process most human beings will experience at some point, and it is a difficult challenge for us all. But we also must determine how to keep going beyond that process. Counseling, support groups, prayer, and other strategies can be very effective.

> At any given point, we can all come up with a list of what we are worried about, what makes us sad, or how life is not fair. No one is immune to those things. However, we can also come up with an even longer list of what we have to be grateful for.

I was only able to have a few consecutive conversations with Susan. But I hope she is able to move beyond this crippling, stagnant point where she cannot proceed with life. Her brother is gone, but she still has other family members who love her and need her to be present with them.

WE ARE ALL UNIQUE

I believe every living adult has gone through some major stress, at least by the time they are in their thirties. But some of those people are more resilient than others, so they have the ability to get through the challenge and get back on track better than others. They are more resilient.

I'm sure we can all relate to these stories, as well as to those of our friends, neighbors, and colleagues. I'll share other stories as we go, but there are many others I can't include in one book, as there are too many accounts. For example, I've known several close friends who lost their homes and all their belongings when a hurricane caused lakes to rise and fill their entire homes with water within a few hours. Can you imagine losing your family's cherished photos, heirlooms that you assumed you would always keep, and all your clothes, furniture, books, and everything you once thought was so important? I frequently see many of those friends who eventually figured out how to resume life and who were able to get past their adversity.

Life stresses will be different for each of us. Some may go through a longer list of challenges than others. But we will all experience *something difficult* at some point in our lives.

Focus on what you are grateful for. There's always something for which we have to be thankful, even when there is pain and great loss.

Chapter 3

WHAT IS RESILIENCE?

A FTER REVIEWING MANY AUTHORS' DEFINITIONS, I CONCLUDED that resilience is the ability to recover from different types of stress, to include physical, mental, or emotional stress. I'll share more definitions and examples along the way.

Different people define resiliency in different ways. Some may call it the ability to recover from adversity. Others may think of it as the ability to accept that change is a part of life and move forward. But it is important to recognize that adversity can also be experienced in everyday challenges as well as in big life hurdles.

Have you ever wondered if some people's brains are wired differently in order to better handle challenges than others? That's what I was wondering, so I started studying more about how the human brain works to get through the toughest challenges, such as loss, grief, and major life obstacles. I learned that there are three main brain regions that play important roles in our ability to be resilient.

The first part of the brain that is significant to a person's resilience is the *prefrontal cortex*. This area of the brain is involved in many brain functions, including executive function, or the ability to self-regulate and to plan our thoughts and actions. Without the complicated actions of our prefrontal cortex, we would have difficulty with abilities such as memory, emotional control, and problem solving. I've worked with patients who had brain injuries, which often damaged their prefrontal cortex. Then it became clear what the role of this frontal lobe region was, since they had significant deficits in their level of brain function. This cortex has also been described as the "personality of the brain." According to Moreno-López (2021), people who are more resilient have greater connectivity between the prefrontal cortex and other areas of the brain that are linked to emotions. These people have less stimulation to their hippocampi and amygdala.[1]

The second brain region significant to resilience is the *hippocampus*. We all have two of these in our brain, and they are responsible for helping us learn, form memories, retrieve memories, as well as achieve other tasks such as spatial processing and navigation. People who are more resilient are said to have greater volumes of gray and white matter in their hippocampi. They also are reported to have greater connectivity between the limbic system and central executive network. The limbic system includes a network of brain areas, such as the amygdala, hippocampus, thalamus, hypothalamus, basal ganglia, and cingulate gyrus. These areas work together to manage our emotions, motivation, memory, and behavior regulation. The central executive network, also known as the lateral frontoparietal network, is mostly made up of the prefrontal cortex, a part of the parietal cortex, and is involved in helping us to have sustained attention, complex problem-solving, and a working memory.[2]

The third significant brain region that plays a role in resilience is the *amygdala* (a-mig'-da-la). This tiny region is only about the size of a shelled peanut but is most significant and very interesting to me!

1. Laura Moreno-López, "What the Distinctive Brains of Resilient People Can Teach Us," *Psyche* (January 13, 2021), https://psyche.co/ideas/what-the-distinctive-brains-of-resilient-people-can-teach-us.

2. Laura Moreno-López, Konstantinos Ioannidis, Adrian Dahl Askelund, Alicia J. Smith, Katja Schueler, Anne-Laura van Harmelen, "The Resilient Emotional Brain: A Scoping Review of the Medial Prefrontal Cortex and Limbic Structure and Function in Resilient Adults With a History of Childhood Maltreatment," *Biological Psychiatry: Cognitive Neuroscience and Neuroimaging* 5, no. 4 (April 2020): 392–402, https://doi.org/10.1016/j.bpsc.2019.12.008.

We have two of these almond-shaped clusters on each side of the brain near the base of the brain. The amygdala plays a huge role in regulating emotions. It also helps us to process information, assess any potential threats, and then make decisions. It also allows us to tie certain emotions to memories. But if not managed, the amygdala has the ability to overthink a situation, causing us to fear the worst-case scenario. Though it is involved in emotions and memory, it is more commonly known for being the center of our fears, due to its key role in our emotions and behaviors. Though we may think of fear as a bad thing, the amygdala plays a big role in our fear related to survival, such as our fight or flight reaction. We also now know that it plays a key role in joyful moments of pleasure and other emotions, so a healthy amygdala is very important to our well-being.

However, the amygdala can become overwhelmed and out of control from stress, anxiety, and panic attacks. According to Perloff (1997), this action has been called an *amygdala hijack*, named by psychologist Daniel Goleman.[3] This overwhelming emotional response overrides a person's rational brain and impairs their ability to think clearly. Think of this as when their fight or flight response kicks in, but there's no actual threat. When this happens, the frontal lobes, which would normally ensure our sense of logic, can no longer allow us to think rationally. Increased amygdala activity, particularly on the left side, is associated with depression. Other disorders such as post-traumatic stress, anxiety disorders, and obsessive-compulsive disorders are also associated with an unhealthy or out-of-control amygdala.

Dr. Goleman also shared the importance of emotional intelligence, including factors related to success. For example, he shared that only 20 percent of a person's practical success is from their intelligence quotient (IQ), while up to 80 percent is from their emotional intelligence (EQ). He shared research on how people with a modest IQ but a higher EQ are often very successful due to their resulting levels of self-control, zeal, persistence, empathy, and ability

---

3. R. Perloff, (1997). "Daniel Goleman's Emotional Intelligence: Why It Can Matter More than IQ [Review of the book *Emotional Intelligence*, by D. Goleman]," *The Psychologist-Manager Journal* 1, no. 1 (1997), 21–22, https://doi.org/10.1037/h0095822.

to motivate others. We now have a great deal of subsequent research on emotional intelligence since these earlier findings, but I find it fascinating to realize the importance of a healthy amygdala.

Scientists who best understand this concept suggest that we must learn to *tame the amygdala* to decrease unnecessary or unknown fears that can otherwise grow out of control, become overwhelming, and decrease our ability to think rationally and to be successful in our quality of life. If we have less connectivity between the amygdala and the ventral default-mode network, which includes several regions that selectively interact to support distinct domains of cognition, then we will have higher resilience.[4] Throughout this book, I'll reference practical ways that we can optimize healthy brain function, and I will share stories of different people who have implemented strategies and actions in order to cultivate their own resilience.

> **We must learn to tame the amygdala to decrease unnecessary or unknown fears that can otherwise grow out of control, become overwhelming, and decrease our ability to think rationally and to be successful in our quality of life.**

Beyond the role of these brain regions, we should also understand the significance of the brain's neurotransmitters. These are the chemical messengers that allow neurons to communicate with each other and with muscles, organs, and glands. Resilience involves more than ten neurotransmitters in the brain, such as dopamine, serotonin, and abrineurin, which is a brain-derived neurotropic factor, or BDNF.[5]

Many people have probably heard about dopamine and serotonin, as they are often discussed when we refer to the *feel-*

---

4. Amber M. Leaver, Hongyu Yang, Prabha Siddarth, Roza M. Vlasova, Beatrix Krause, Natalie St. Cyr, Katherine L. Narr, Helen Lavretsky, "Resilience and Amygdala Function in Older Healthy and Depressed Adults," *Journal of Affective Disorders* 237 (April 2018): 27–34.

5. Carlos Osório, Thomas Probert, Edgar Jones, Allan H. Young, Ian Robbins, "Adapting to Stress: Understanding the Neurobiology of Resilience," *Behavioral Medicine* 43, no. 4 (April 21, 2016): 307–322.

good chemicals in the brain. Dopamine is involved in movement, coordination, and feelings of pleasure and reward. Serotonin is associated with feelings of happiness, focus, and calm, and can affect digestion and metabolism. When serotonin or dopamine levels drop, the results can lead to depression, anger, pain, or other conditions.

I am most intrigued by BDNF, which is a protein in the brain. When we have higher BDNF, we have improved cognition, new brain cells stay alive and flourish, we have lower depression rates, and we may even experience decreased effects of aging. Scientists call BDNF the "Miracle-Gro for the brain." The more I study BDNF, the more I realize it may be one of the most critical factors to build resilience. Smart advertising may promote certain pills as helping to build cognitive function, but a close analysis of these supplements shows their goal is to increase BDNF. Yet the most significant and proven method of increasing BDNF in the brain is consistent exercise. This factor is covered in more detail in the section on physical resilience.

How do these brain factors affect our ability to experience or respond to stress? Well, first it's important to know that everyone experiences stress in a similar manner. No one is immune to the experience. And everyone has a certain response to stress. But the person with more resilience will adapt better following the stress. They have more of their brain working to adapt to the situation through what we call *ongoing plasticity*. In other words, there is an ongoing, flexible adaptive process helping us to recover from the toughest challenge and then regroup to move forward following the stress.[6]

> No one is immune to the experience. And everyone has a certain response to stress. But the person with more resilience will adapt better following the stress.

In addition to the way our brains work differently to respond to stress, there are several other factors that also play a role in how

---

6. Richard G. Hunter, Jason D. Gray, and Bruce S. McEwen, "The Neuroscience of Resilience," *Journal of the Society for Social Work and Research* 9, no. 2 (2018): 305–339.

we respond and adapt to stress. Other significant factors include a person's family genetics, their environment, their unique personality traits, their level of cardiorespiratory and physical fitness, and their family and level of social support. That is why you may see that one person responds to stress as a challenge, but another person thinks the same stress is a serious threat to their life, which they may not be able to handle.

When a person builds resiliency and learns to manage their stress, they can then work to improve their performance at work or in other areas of life.

Therefore, when a person builds resiliency and learns to manage their stress, they can then work to improve their performance at work or in other areas of life. But when they perceive stress as a threat, it can then have a significant negative effect on their physical and mental health.[7] The good news is that there is significant evidence supporting how we can use strategies to build the muscle of resilience.[8]

Dr. Rashmi Parmar, a psychiatrist with Mindpath Health, recommends the following strategies to build resilience:

- *Keep the brain engaged.* When we seek new cognitive activities and challenges, we activate parts of our brain that are otherwise dormant. This increases the neural network that leads to the improved ability for positive coping mechanisms.

- *Choose optimism.* Change how you think about the situation. For example, if I look at it from a different angle, I might find a silver lining in an otherwise bad situation.

- *Develop a problem-solving attitude.* For example, I will take on this new, seemingly impossible challenge; if I fail along the way, I could also learn from the process.

- *Spend time focusing on purpose.* What is meaningful to me? My overall well-being and health are priorities, along with

---

7. Rashmi Parmar, "What Can We Learn about Resilience from Senior Citizens?" *Psychiatric Times* 39, no. 5 (2022): 32–33.

8. Moreno-López, "What the Distinctive Brains."

other points that matter most to me. This will be slightly different for us all.

- *Surround yourself with supportive friends.* This may be one or two people or several close friends. Nurture these positive relationships that bring you strength.

- *Build confidence.* We can challenge ourselves with tasks that push us beyond our level of comfort, but that will not threaten our peace of mind.

- *Put your situation in perspective.* When we reach out to help others who are also living with challenges, it often helps us to realize we're not the only one; in fact, many others are living with greater challenges than our own.

- *Build a resilient body.* A healthy diet and active lifestyle support and allow a resilient mind.

- *Practice mindfulness.* Focus on the present with kindness and nonjudgement. Examples of mindful practices include breathing strategies, meditation, prayer, yoga, and tai chi, though there are many others. So find what works for you.[9]

Now that we have the definitions and strategies for resilience, let's look at the different types of resilience. The four main types are physical resilience, mental resilience, emotional resilience, and social resilience. We will review a little information about each one, since the optimal plan would be the combined efforts for all.

PHYSICAL RESILIENCE

Physical resilience focuses on how the body deals with change—to recover from physical demands, illnesses, and injuries. Research supports the idea that this type of resilience plays an important role in health. It affects how people age as well as how they respond and recover from physical stress and medical issues. This type of resilience is something that a person can improve, to a certain extent, by making healthy lifestyle choices. For example, one could focus

---

9. Parmar, "What Can We Learn."

on getting enough sleep, eating a nutritious diet, and engaging in regular exercise to strengthen this type of resilience.[10]

Consider how the process of weightlifting can build resilience. I've worked with gym circuit machines for this type of exercise, thinking I was doing something good for my body. But a few different times in my life, I've worked with a personal trainer for a couple of months at a time, such as after having both of my children. Each trainer pushed me harder than I ever would have known was possible. During that one hour of doing whatever they instructed me to do, it felt impossible, but I got through it. When I left the gym, I could hardly walk, and forty-eight hours later I would be so extremely sore I couldn't even sit or turn over in bed without screaming in pain. But this form of physical stress can lead to improved physical and mental strength if managed appropriately, which includes adequate recovery between sessions.

By consistently challenging your body with weights and allowing it to recover, you're not only building muscle but also enhancing your body's ability to bounce back from various types of stress. In other words, your body is becoming stronger and more resilient.[11]

This process of adapting to stress contributes to overall resilience, which is then beneficial for both physical and mental health. But it's important to balance the stress of weightlifting with proper nutrition, hydration, and rest to ensure the best results and avoid overtraining. Both scientific studies and anecdotal stories from individuals have shown that physical exercise often leads to greater brain activity, to include a sharper focus, greater memory, and even decreased effects of aging.

Other scientific studies have described resilience as the outcome of a dynamic process of adaptation in the face of adversity and changing demands. It is reported that people with high resilience

10. Heather E. Whitson, Wei Duan-Porter, Kenneth E. Schmader, Miriam C. Morey, Harvey J. Cohen, Cathleen S. Colón-Emeric, "Physical Resilience in Older Adults: Systematic Review and Development of an Emerging Construct," *Journals of Gerontology Series A: Biological Sciences and Medical* Sciences 71, no. 4 (April 2016): 489–95, doi:10.1093/gerona/glv202.

11. Michal Krzysztofik, Michal Wilk, Grzegorz Wojdała, and Artur Gołaś, "Maximizing Muscle Hypertrophy: A Systematic Review of Advanced Resistance Training Techniques and Methods," *International Journal of Environmental Research and Public Health* 16, no. 24 (2019): 4897, https://doi.org/10.3390/ijerph16244897.

are less likely to develop mental health problems in proportion to the accumulated stressor load.[12] In other words, the complex and ongoing response to stress leads to greater abilities or resiliency.

Neumann et. al (2021) shares several cross-sectional and longitudinal field studies that conclude that the protective, stress-buffering effects of exercise and fitness have been associated with a better capacity to cope with chronic stress, fewer health complaints, and higher self-perceived resilience.[13]

Physical exercise often leads to greater brain activity, to include a sharper focus, greater memory, and even decreased effects of aging.

Another type of physical activity reported to result in resiliency is interval training. Interval training involves alternating periods of activity and recovery. This type of training has been used by athletes to enhance performance for over a century and has been proven to induce remarkable physiological adaptations and health benefits. Physiological adaptations required by interval training is not only due to intensity but also to the nature of the intermittent levels of exercise.[14]

12. Raffael Kalisch, Dewleen G. Baker, Ulrike Basten, Marco P. Boks, George A. Bonanno, Eddie Brummelman, Andrea Chmitorz, Guillén Fernàndez, Christian J. Fiebach, Isaac Galatzer-Levy, Elbert Geuze, Sergiu Groppa, Isabella Helmreich, Talma Hendler, Erno J. Hermans, Tanja Jovanovic, Thomas Kubiak, Klaus Lieb, Beat Lutz, Marianne B. Müller, Ryan J. Murray, Caroline M. Nievergelt, Andreas Reif, Karin Roelofs, Bart P. F. Rutten, David Sander, Anita Schick, Oliver Tüscher, Ilse Van Diest, Anne-Laura van Harmelen, Ilya M. Veer, Eric Vermetten, Christiaan H. Vinkers, Tor D. Wager, Henrik Walter, Michèle Wessa, Michael Wibral, and Birgit Kleim, "The Resilience Framework as a Strategy to Combat Stress-Related Disorders," *Nature Human Behavior* 1 (October 16, 2017), nature.com. https://www.nature.com/articles/s41562-017-0200-8.

13. R. J. Neumann, K. F. Ahrens, B. Kollmann, N. Goldbach, A. Chmitorz, D. Weichert, C. J. Fiebach, M. Wessa, R. Kalisch, K. Lieb, O. Tüscher, M. M. Plichta, A. Reif, and S. Matura, "The Impact of Physical Fitness on Resilience to Modern Life Stress and the Mediating Role of General Self-Efficacy," *European Archives of Psychiatry and Clinical Neuroscience* 272 (October 7, 2021): 679–692, https://doi.org/10.1007/s00406-021-01338-9.

14. Muhammed Mustafa Atakan, Yanchun Li, Şükran Nazan Koşar, Hüseyin Hüsrev Turnagöl, and Xu Yan, "Evidence-Based Effects of High-Intensity Interval Training on Exercise Capacity and Health: A Review with Historical Perspective," *International Journal of Environmental Research and Public Health* 18, no. 13 (July 5, 2021): 7201, https://doi.org/10.3390/ijerph18137201.

I've been reading applications of such research from performance psychologists and researchers Jim Loehr and Tony Schwartz, who utilize athletic concepts to help people in the workforce become high performers, utilizing more energy to achieve results through recovery times. This concept applies to all of us who are workaholics to learn how taking breaks and adding physical training and life balance helps us to achieve more outcomes than when we work nonstop without breaks. Loehr and Schwartz (2003) stated, "Interval training is a means to build more energy capacity and to tolerate more stress, but also to teach the body to recover more efficiently."[15]

MENTAL RESILIENCE

Mental resilience is a person's ability to adapt to change as well as to unknown situations. When a person has this type of resilience, they may be more flexible, rational, and calm during times of crisis. They can think creatively and can adapt to the new and changing situations to still achieve goals and move forward. The person with mental resilience is able to use this mental strength to solve complex problems and to maintain hope despite their significant challenges. Many of the rewards discussed above in physical resilience often lead to greater mental resilience.

EMOTIONAL RESILIENCE

Emotional resilience refers to a person's ability to regulate emotions during times of stress. This relates back to the EQ we recently discussed. Resilient people are aware of their emotional reactions and are often more in touch with their inner life. Because of this, they are often better equipped to calm their mind and to manage their emotions when they are dealing with negative stresses. This type of resilience supports a person's ability to maintain some sense of optimism, even through great levels of adversity. Because they are emotionally resilient, they understand that this tough period of life will not last forever.

---

15. Jim Loehr and Tony Schwartz, *The Power of Full Engagement: Managing Energy, Not Time, Is the Key to High Performance and Personal Renewal* (NY: Free Press, 2003).

SOCIAL RESILIENCE

Social resilience occurs when groups of people work together to recover from difficult situations. It includes people working together to solve problems that affect people both individually and collectively. An example of this in my part of the world includes the response to the aftermath of destructive hurricanes. People lost their homes, pets, and family members. They were often left with almost nothing, but watching the community rally together to donate clothes, money, and food was such a beautiful thing to witness. Then others, who may have also lost everything, would show up to work on rebuilding the houses of people they had never met. It was amazing in my own neighborhood following Hurricane Harvey to watch people come together with others who would have otherwise never even known one another. Everyone did what they could to help one another. It was a type of healing for the entire community.

Incorporate strategies for physical, mental, emotional, and social resilience. This could be as simple as adding more movement and activity to each day. Then try something new and reach out to help others.

Chapter 4

EARLY UNIVERSITY CHALLENGES

I WAS THE FIRST PERSON IN MY FAMILY TO ATTEND COLLEGE, BUT I didn't realize the significance of the "first generation" thing until several decades later when I heard through my professional organizations that there are entire clubs and scholarships for what they now call *first-generation college students*. I just knew all throughout high school that of course I would go to college. It never occurred to me that because my parents, brother, and sister didn't go to college it would be a whole new ball game. I was determined to figure it out one step at a time. And though my dad was my biggest source of encouragement, my mom worried about me. She also didn't want me to leave home and begged me to stay and work at the bank like *normal people* from our small town.

The biggest struggle was when I realized my first year that I didn't have the type of brain that could be successful at engineering. My high school physics and calculus teacher convinced us this was the best career for all of us in his class. So I chose Louisiana Tech University since, at the time, it was the only school that offered biomedical engineering. I was most interested in the medical field, and this degree plan would merge my interests with what my calculus teacher said was the best career plan.

When I got to college, ready to excel in all my engineering courses, I found myself in class in a large auditorium. My professor walked in and wrote formulas all over the many chalkboards, murmuring while he spoke and never even turning to look at the class. I looked around the room full of mostly males rapidly taking notes and looking at their complex calculators. When I tried talking to them, I learned many were from other countries, and they mostly had two or three calculus classes in high school. But I had only taken the first calculus class, so I had no idea what this professor was talking about.

Now that my son is about to graduate with an engineering degree, I have learned that most engineering students need all these courses in high school or they teach themselves from online resources after they get to the large engineering universities. Then, when they take the courses in college, they prove on the tests what they have learned on their own. My son also thinks in complex mathematical terms, and my brain never worked that way. Maybe things would have been different if I had gone to a smaller private university where professors have smaller classes and actually make eye contact? But then again, that would have changed my course in life, which was not meant to be, as I later found a better fit for my innate abilities.

Since I had thought I could achieve anything when I first arrived on campus, I felt a great sense of failure when I realized I needed to change my major to something else. I proceeded to change majors several more times until I felt like I had finally found my calling and purpose. I liked something about each of my majors, but then I would hear about another major I didn't even know about and would move on to that plan. Because of all these changes, I was also always trying to catch up with the needed extra hours. That means I took more than a full load every quarter, which was the Louisiana Tech University version of a semester.

I learned many other life lessons in college. For example, at the beginning of my freshman year, I was in a speech class (because of course I love public speaking) when Barry Brantley, the coach from the Louisiana Tech speech and debate team, came to visit and tell us about their club. The second that class was over, I went straight to Robinson Hall to sign up. The thought of traveling around the country to compete by delivering speeches sounded too good to be true! I started by planning to compete in the different categories, such as informative speeches, persuasive speeches, impromptu speeches, and even excerpts of dramatic plays. Then Barry convinced me to add debate to my roster. I decided to try it because it could be another great opportunity. But I failed miserably. It was beyond embarrassing, and, to this day, I feel bad for my debate partner, who watched me bomb our chances of advancing to the next level.

I later realized I was amongst all the skillful pre-law students, and apparently a prerequisite to success is appearing to be obnoxious with the ability to belittle and prove the opposing team to be wrong. I do not have such abilities and cannot even pretend to be that person. Instead, I wanted to be the peacemaker and agree with some of their points while being too gentle with my own side of the argument. That is not how a debate is supposed to go!

From that point on, I became more cognizant of my strengths and weaknesses and stuck with the individual speaking events. My team members, however, never let me live down this failure. In fact, when I was a junior, I was elected president of the speech and debate team—or Pi Kappa Delta, its honorary fraternity name. The role of president included a small quarterly scholarship for leadership. But a friend and senior on the team, Jackie Taylor, was quick to point out, "That just means they pay you *not* to debate."

> **From that point on, I became more cognizant of my strengths and weaknesses.**

I learned other lessons, including all the reasons I should not major in certain subjects. Changing my major so many times (including chemistry, pre-pharmacy, dietetics, education, graphic design, communications, marketing, and speech education) required a lot of paperwork and appointments at the dean's office, among other things. Though I liked some components of each and still incorporate many of them into areas of my current work, none of them were the perfect fit for me. Some were too difficult, while others were too easy and not challenging enough. Friends at school and in my hometown began to laugh at my indecisiveness. It was hard not to feel like a failure.

Then one day, while we were in the speech and debate team van, heading to some other state to compete for the weekend, I saw something of interest. Barry couldn't go on that trip, so he asked a fellow graduate student in his department to go in his place. It was a girl who was a graduate assistant in speech language pathology. Today the major is called *communication disorders* or *speech, hearing, and science disorders*. She brought her books in the van to study, and I started asking her questions about this degree plan. By the time we arrived at our destination, I was convinced that this was my calling in life. It meant I would need to get my master's degree before I could get the needed certification to work, but I didn't care. However, when I called to tell my mother, she said, "Let me get this straight. You are finally going to graduate at some point, but you can't do anything with your degree until you get another degree?" I responded, "Yes! But it's going to be great!"

GRADUATE SCHOOL

So many things that we want do in life, decisions we make, and initiatives we need choose to pursue, could make or break our major ability to function in life. But we have to just take a breath, plan for the best, trust our instincts to prepare for this moment, and then go for it.

Planning for graduate school added another level of stress. First, I needed financial help, but the most significant factor determining who would receive the scholarship was the Graduate Record Exam (GRE). I heard horror stories of how impossible this test would be. I studied the practice tests and did the best I could to prepare. Going into the test, I felt a great deal of anxiety, thinking about how this four-hour test would decide my future. If you think too much about that, it could completely overwhelm your brain from working.

On a sidenote, let's just consider the lesson here. So many things that we want do in life, decisions we make, and initiatives we need choose to pursue, could make or break our major ability to function in life. But we have to just take a breath, plan for the best, trust our instincts to prepare for this moment, and then go for it. You can't give up and decide it is too difficult. The brain can be completely crippled with fear. That is because when we think too much about the *what if it is too difficult?* then we allow our amygdala to take over, which then lets fear outweigh our abilities to function.

I finished the GRE and knew that some questions were so impossible that my responses were only my best guess. Back then, the GRE General Test included three subtests: verbal reasoning, quantitative reasoning, and analytical writing. Prior to 2011, each subtest used a scoring scale of 200–800, whereas the new GRE scale uses 130–170. Nowadays, everything is quickly scored, with results posted online. Back then we had to wait several weeks for our scores, and even then, test results were mailed to our campus mailbox. My waiting period for those scores that would determine my future included great anxiety.

Finally I received word from a classmate that the scores had been mailed, but I was on a semester break in my hometown of DeRidder, LA, which was three hours away from the campus post office. So my friend Katie Anderson rode with me for the long, three-hour drive so I could get my test scores. When I arrived and opened the envelope, I was shocked. It was confusing, but I was pretty sure I had failed the test and my life was over. *What would I do with an undergraduate degree that meant nothing without a master's degree?* With this low score, I couldn't even get into a graduate school, much less get a scholarship to pay for it.

I hardly spoke to Katie all the way home. I couldn't even say out loud how desolate and hopeless I felt. Two weeks later, my classmate and dear friend, Deanna Roberts, had also just received her scores. She called me from Baton Rouge to ask how I did on the test. I burst into tears and said, "Deanna, I think I failed! My life is over!" But then she said, "Well, what were your combined scores, and what did you make on the first section?" Wait, what? I was supposed to add the scores? I had only looked at one of the three scores, thinking it was the total score or maybe an average score. So I thought I made 400 instead of the needed 1,100. But there was no total score line on the paper. I asked for clarification, and she explained that your GRE score is the total of all three scores. What a giant relief!

It turned out that I did well enough to get into any grad school. I also received a full scholarship to Memphis State University, which was my top school pick since it was a medical-based program. I thought about all those weeks living in fear, waiting for the *what if?* Then finally getting the answer and misunderstanding it, spending another two weeks thinking my life was over. What a waste of time and energy!

I arrived in Memphis the following June to begin my graduate school program, and I soon realized this would be more physically and mentally exhausting than I could have ever imagined. We had a small cohort of classmates who would start together, since we were beginning our program in the summer semester rather than waiting for the larger fall semester group to start. The program had very high standards for the students they accepted, and those that they did choose were all on scholarships and stipends. We soon learned there would be high pressure in this *sink or swim* fight.

We would mostly see clients all day, then take afternoon and evening classes, then go home to study all night and be back in therapy sessions the next morning at 8 a.m. I had chosen a safe place to live that was thirty-to-forty minutes away, depending on time of day and traffic. So the commute was harder than expected. Our professors were all well-known across the country, as they were well-published authors and editors of books and professional journals. It was an honor to be in their classes, but the tests were harder than anything we had ever done. If you overprepared and studied every resource possible, you could make the required B or above. But when someone made a *C*, they were pulled aside, counseled that they didn't have what it takes, and were sent home/kicked out of the program. No questions asked, no second chances. And that is just how it worked.

In retrospect, if the professors and clinical supervisors had made it more bearable, it wouldn't have been a major accomplishment to survive the program. The hours were long, with every moment utilized for studying, seeing clients, or attending class. There was very little time left to sleep or do anything else. We lived in fear that we wouldn't make the grade. They reiterated that only the best would survive this program. I lived on minimal sleep. One day I counted the cups of coffee I was drinking and realized I was averaging fourteen cups a day! And I was eating only whatever was fast.

After two years of intensive stress, my body responded in strange ways: all my eyelashes fell out, I got vocal nodules, and I felt as though I was physically falling apart. But the point is, I survived! I'm now thankful that my professors didn't *dumb it down* and that they pushed us to succeed. I also know the reward of graduating from that intense experience would be a foundation for many other successes in life.

Realize that when one door closes, another one opens. Anticipate the great rewards for getting through the most challenging situations.

Chapter 5

LEARNING TO RUN

I *CAN'T BREATHE. MY BODY IS SCREAMING AT ME TO FALL ON THE GROUND and collapse. My legs are throbbing. I may throw up or pass out. Why am I doing this? Oh God, help me!* These were my only thoughts while I was attempting to run.

By the end of graduate school, I knew I needed to work on my health. I tried taking a few minutes each day to run around the block near my apartment. This was not a successful venture. I could barely jog for ten minutes and would end up walking. Then one day I was talking to George Lee Glass, my friend and youth pastor at church. He told me to meet him the next morning at 6:15 a.m. and we would run together. You know that dual feeling of excitement about a goal that's finally going to happen with a friend's help, along with the sheer fear of the anticipated pain and agony all at the same time? That was my state of thought.

I showed up the next morning, a bit sleepy but mistakenly feeling slightly *athletic*. Nothing could be further from the truth. I had felt a bit of success at my new job and in other ventures, but physical fitness had never been one of them.

That first day was the most excruciating, impossible feat. I lasted about ten minutes in what I would now call a slow jog before I thought I was going to collapse, throw up, or just die. But my new running partner coached me through it and would not let me stop. By some miracle I made it the entire two-mile trek. I'm sure he was wondering what impossible commitment he agreed to when promising to help me. For the rest of that day my legs felt severe levels of pain, I could barely walk, and I also wondered if this was going to work. The next morning my alarm went off again at 5:30 a.m. I got up, drank a cup of coffee, rubbed pain cream on my throbbing legs, and left at 6:05 a.m. to go meet him for more torture. It did not get easier. It was the entire scenario all over again.

The following days and weeks included great struggles. Though my new running partner was right by my side, he never let me stop to walk it out so I could get my breath. My legs were burning, I could barely breathe, my lungs were struggling. I wanted to throw up and collapse all at the same time. We ran two miles every morning. I needed ibuprofen during the day just to walk down the hall to see clients, and I woke up early every morning to put menthol cream on my legs and stretch before the run just to get them to work again.

I asked my running partner, who seemed to have done this all of his life and appeared to know all the answers to this running thing, "Will this ever get easier?" I was hoping for great words of encouragement. But he said, "No." Then he added, "Not for a while, but then one day, when you least expect it, you will be able to breathe while running." So I continued this excruciating event each morning. At the time, I was also singing at church with the worship team, and Darryl Dotson, our music director, gave us tapes every week to learn before practice. One morning, I decided that one of the songs I was learning would be my inspiration to get me through this torture. So, while driving to meet George Lee for our morning run, I listened to the song "When the Battle Is Over" to prepare my thoughts and body for this grueling experience. The words stuck in my head and encouraged me:

> Don't wait 'til the battle is over, shout now!
> You know in the end you're gonna win! . . .
> Gonna thank Him for the rain,

Gonna thank Him for the pain,
Gonna thank Him for the trials, He brought me through,
Gonna thank him when I'm happy.
Gonna thank him when I'm sad.
Hallelujah![16]

The song was invigorating, and if you've ever heard the Walter Hawkins singers, you know how fun they are. So it brought me joy!

Then, a few weeks into this new morning ritual, I arrived to start the run and felt like I could actually breathe and make it to the end of our two miles! Oh, thank God! Then George Lee said, "Today we're going two and a half miles." *What?! Ugh!* After a week surviving that adjustment, he announced, "Today we're going three miles." Eventually he increased the plan to three and a half miles. Each increase in distance meant a new struggle to breathe along with burning leg muscles. But somehow, I survived!

In retrospect, I now realize that George Lee was more of a coach than a running partner. He pushed me to my limits every day but also probably kept me from a complete cardiac event in going beyond my limits. For example, once I could sustain my breath for the entire run, he set a new rule. Near the end of the run, with about two-tenths of a mile to go, he would say, "Now we're going to sprint! Push it with everything you've got!" Then after about five hundred feet he would say, "Now faster!" At that point I thought I was the fastest person alive as I had never done anything like this in my life. It was super hard, but I knew I only had to survive a few more feet and then I could collapse on the ground of the driveway, our destination point.

Another thing he did for the last few months was push me to increase my speed. I was finally comfortable jogging my slow nine-minute mile, talking most of the way with him in sync beside me. I always showed up with an inspiring quote, and we exchanged stories because of course I like to talk! He started speeding three feet in front of me the entire time. So the only way I could talk or share a story was to speed up as well! We worked our way to achieving eight-and-a-half-minute miles. I would have never managed that speed when running alone.

---

16. Donald Lawrence, "When the Battle Is Over," from the album Your Righteous Mind (2011).

It is important to say, looking back, that at some point (months later), I did enjoy the run. I felt really great afterwards—going home, taking a shower, getting dressed for work, and in a great mood all day to cheer up my nursing home residents. Since I enjoy talking so much, I would have a quote or poem for the day or research to cite, or we would even discuss goals for our church youth group. I could breathe well enough to talk and run at the same time!

Eventually George Lee moved away to another ministry job, but I continued my daily runs and enjoyed that for many decades. I replaced the running buddy concept with a headset and then earbuds. Sometimes I ran slower but longer five-to-eight-mile treks, and sometimes I ran a faster two-mile trek, depending on how fast I needed to be finished, dressed, and at work.

I have many times applied that experience to a goal that seems to be above my own physical capabilities. I really wanted to stop or come up with an excuse to miss a day. But we ran through the rain, snow, and all temperatures—from the melting one-hundred-degree weather to some winter days in the below-freezing, twenty-degree weather. Many times at least one of us probably had minimal sleep the night before, and the conditions were rarely ideal. But we did it.

There were no days to sleep in or take the day off. I referred to it then as discipline, but now I think of it more as perseverance.

There were no days to sleep in or take the day off. I referred to it then as discipline, but now I think of it more as perseverance. Every day I showed up in the parsonage driveway, and every day he came outside. And our day began.

I should clarify that my journey regarding exercise started much later in life. Since I was diagnosed with scoliosis at the age of ten, the orthopedic physician at the time explained many exercise restrictions to my mother. (On an unrelated note, during that visit with the orthopedic physician, picture my Pentecostal mother's silent anger and changed facial expression when the doctor told her that humans were never supposed to walk on two legs but that we were meant to still be monkeys, walking on four legs. He was an atheist and was adamant about sharing his beliefs. My mother could barely hold it together. God bless her!) The exercise precautions given by the orthopedic physician would be completely different now, as we know that exercise is good for the spine. But the restrictions at that time were so severe that it was enough for me to not be able to take PE class like my friends. He did say swimming was allowed, but I didn't know how to swim, and my mother was terrified that I would drown, so she did not allow me to go near the water. That's another story for the next chapter.

Given the doctor's orders not to exercise, much of my middle school and high school years were spent without much-needed exercise. Rather than taking PE and participating in sports like normal teenagers, I spent that extra time doing science projects, helping teachers, and cramming in as many extra academics or club responsibilities as possible. As a result, I was always carrying a little extra weight and was not reaping the excellent benefits of exercise that I now know is so critical.

I read a lot about health and nutrition in college. I tried supplemental herbal drinks and finally took an aerobics class in college. But I would need much more than that to get me to where I needed to be. In graduate school, I found it interesting that many of my professors were distance runners. So I tried to run when time allowed, mostly on the weekends, but I could barely achieve a slow mile. Thus, this opportunity to have a running partner was exactly what I needed to push me to new levels of fitness that seemed otherwise impossible.

This experience made me a better person in so many areas. When I was in my twenties, I only wanted to lose weight. I knew a little bit about the stress-relief benefits of exercise, but I had no idea about the many other far-reaching benefits of running and cardiorespiratory fitness. Now, when I teach successful aging initiatives to health care professionals and caregivers, I remind them that weight loss is really a side benefit. The more important benefit of exercise includes brain function and what I've now experienced as physical, mental, and emotional resilience. Research shows and is validated by what I see in myself, my clients, and my colleagues, that the effects of exercise can achieve the following:

- Improved brain function
- Decreased stress
- Enhanced hippocampus
- Neurogenesis (brain cells born every day)
- Improved brain cell survival rate

- Improved performance on long-term memory tasks
- Increased frontal lobe function (attention)
- Increased production of endorphins, dopamine, and serotonin
- Improved mood, long-term memory, and clarity of mind
- Thicker brain cortex, more blood vessels, and more positive neurotransmitters like acetylcholine
- Improved heart and lung function
- Improved quality of sleep
- Improved balance/resilience
- Lower risk for major threat of disease

In addition to these improved health benefits, my body changed! I had attempted diets all through high school and college in my attempt to get below a certain size. But after starting that painful run one October morning, in March I went shopping for a dress to wear for our church Easter program. I tried a size smaller than my typical, and it was too big! I tried a size even smaller, and it was too big. The next size down fit perfectly! I was so busy getting through each long day that I had not even realized this extra benefit. I know that sounds crazy, but I had found a good seamstress lady who would periodically alter my clothes to make them fit better. I just had no idea how much my body was changing.

I can now reflect on many applications of resilience to this personal experience. Nothing about those first few months was easy or enjoyable. Every day I wanted to quit and say, "Well, at least I tried." There were tears and frustrations, pain and nausea. But each day was a new opportunity to rise to the occasion, psych myself up for the agony and pain I was about to experience, then make it through this struggle, which would take everything I had in me just to get through. Surviving that physical adversity helped me develop physical resilience, which meant I was stronger to handle more intensity—or what used to feel like adversity. My body could now handle more. What had once felt like the greatest trial was now an enjoyable experience.

Honestly, I was so busy trying to survive, especially those first few weeks, that I probably did not appreciate the coaching and friendship of George Lee. He never let me stop moving forward.

One day in those first two weeks, I was gasping for breath and begged, "Please let me stop! I can't go any further!" I expected his normal response of, "Just keep going; you can do this." Instead, he said, "OK." I looked at him in shock and said, "Really?" He continued, "If you have to stop, then stop. I'll keep going and then get the Jeep to come back and get you." So of course I did not stop and made it to the end. He knew my limits more than I did. I'm now forever grateful for my friend who stuck with me, though he did not have to deal with my woes. Of course, some days I secretly hoped he would oversleep and not come outside so I could go home and take a break! But he *always* showed up.

There were tears and frustrations, pain and nausea. But each day was a new opportunity to rise to the occasion, psych myself up for the agony and pain I was about to experience, then make it through this struggle.

Friends are amazing. I've had many life stresses since then, with different friends helping me through different life battles. They are there when needed but also give us space when needed. They offer support but do not give unsolicited advice. So, from this story about learning to run, I gained the ability to exercise, which became a critical resource for future resilience and strength. I learned the power of a friend to be there to get me through it. And there would be many other times that other good friends would be there to get me through new challenges.

You may never know what you're capable of doing until you step out of your comfort zone. Get a friend to push you, or take a class. Seek the support you need, but make it happen! Just get through it for one day, then again the next day, and the next . . . until it's a daily practice.

Chapter 6

LEARNING TO DIVE

T HE ICY WATER WAS FREEZING. THE OUTSIDE TEMPERATURE WAS twenty-eight degrees, and there was ice and snow on the ground. I had just jumped into Lake Travis in Austin, Texas, to go down thirty feet in dark, muddy water where I couldn't see anything and had to stay down there for twenty minutes. The double neoprene wetsuit did not seem to help prevent hypothermia. I wore my oxygen tanks and buoyancy control device (BCD) to breathe, and I had a compass to prove that I could find my way back to the boat. However, I'd never been good at determining directions, so how was a compass going to help? It just told me how to find *north*.

Diving was supposed to be an amazing experience where you could see coral reefs, swim with beautiful marine life, and feel at peace with nature. So far, my entire body was shaking uncontrollably in the frigid, dark water. I was afraid of dying. I had no idea how to get back to the safe boat after twenty minutes, and the only things I'd seen through the dark, muddy water were remnants of an old, rusted lawn chair sitting on the bottom of the lake.

This *learning to dive* thing was a last-minute idea, which is why I didn't take the normal route to learn to dive in the warm summer with a class of other people. A friend was visiting in December and said, "Hey, we can get cheap flights and a hotel in Cozumel in January; let's get a group together and go!" The problem was that everyone else in the group had their diving certification. I decided I would go on this trip as well, but I would first need to quickly get my certification to not miss out on anything. There were a few problems with this plan. First of all, I can't swim.

That's right. My mother was always afraid I would drown yet wouldn't allow me to take lessons to learn how to swim. Instead, she just decided to keep me away from water. Her paranoia of losing me and her overprotectiveness stemmed from the fact that she had two babies born prior to my older sister, both of whom died before they were one year old. The first died from pneumonia when the doctor assured her it was just a bad cold. The second died of a collapsed lung at birth, though he still lived five months. From that point on, I believe my mother had mental health struggles, for which she should have received counseling. She often tried to talk me out of every challenging initiative that I chose to pursue throughout my life. Due to her own fears, she always wanted me to take the safe option. I was involved in every club possible at school and in every church activity. Then I wanted to go to college three hours away, and I chose a graduate school thirteen hours away. My mother begged me not to do any of those things. Fortunately my father was very encouraging and wanted me to do everything I wanted to do. But the fact remained that I was never allowed to learn to swim.

The requirements for diving certification included the equivalent of two weeks of classroom training to learn all the rules. *That's fine. I can definitely do that!* The next step was pool work, including swimming for two hundred yards. I was being overly optimistic when I told myself, *I can learn, right?* The diving instructor gave me an address to meet him at a pool where the next lesson would take place. It was a large, outdoor pool, but it had a roof over it, and the water was heated. The outside temperature was in the low thirties, but the water was heated and felt warm. *OK, I can do this!*

The instructor showed me how to put on the weight belt, the snorkel, and all the gear; then he instructed me to go sit on the bottom of a twelve-foot pool. Once I was there, I would need to take off my breathing apparatus (mask, BC, oxygen, etc.) and weights and lay them down beside me, proving I could stay in control of the situation and continue to be able to hold my breath. Then, I would need to figure out how to pick up the equipment from the floor of the pool and put it all back on without taking a breath and without panicking. Recall that I was never allowed to be close to any body of water growing up. As a result, I've always been terrified to be near any body of even shallow water, as I did not have the skills to swim or survive in that unknown world. I was also afraid I might miss some of my guide's instructions, since he gave all this verbal information to me while we were standing out of the pool where it was very cold, and I was shivering. And now I was supposed to sit twelve feet below water without an oxygen mask and somehow remain calm. The pool water was heated, but it was still an outdoor pool. As I mentioned, normal people take diving classes in the summer.

So I sat at the bottom of that twelve-foot pool with no BC. If I panicked and chose to inhale, I would die! But somehow, I got through it. After a successful demonstration that I could remove all gear and put it back on without breathing, I felt a huge victory. I was shocked at my ability to do this. I passed the test! How in the world was that possible? I was the girl who couldn't swim, and now I had just sat at the bottom of the pool without any equipment, and I did not die!

After that day, I began to think differently. About everything. I had just conquered my greatest fear. That meant that now I could conquer any other challenge that I thought may have been impossible. *What else have I been afraid of? What else should I try that I always thought was impossible? I can do anything!*

Then it was time to swim two hundred yards and then tread water or float for a full five minutes. Well, after the victory of sitting under twelve feet of water, I was ready to figure out how to do it. Fortunately this poor guy who had agreed to be my diving instructor in the freezing winter had other superpowers. He recently had a job teaching preschoolers how to swim at the YMCA. How lucky for me! So he proceeded to walk me through a quick crash course on how to swim. When I couldn't make the full two hundred yards, which was many laps from one end to the other, he let me start over. Finally I did it! I couldn't tread water long enough, as I seemed to panic for a moment, and by that time my body felt too much fatigue. But I did eventually float for ten minutes with good breathing and relaxation techniques, so that worked enough to pass the last pool test.

After passing all of these confined water dive tests, I was now ready to meet the next day for two twenty-minute open water dives in Lake Travis. I really thought the pool tests were the hardest part since I would have oxygen tanks on my back for the open water part, so I wouldn't have to worry about drowning. But that night, we had a snow/ice storm. Prior to that day, I do not ever remember an ice storm in Austin, Texas! *Why today?!*

I barely got my car out of the iced driveway without crashing it into a tree and slowly inched my way to the marina near my house. No one else even seemed to venture out on the roads that day, much less jump into the freezing lake. The divemaster was there along with the driver of a heated houseboat. I think they both worried that I would die of hypothermia. They gave me an additional and thicker wetsuit to wear over the full-body wetsuit I was already wearing. After finally getting the thing on, I could barely move. The instructor told me to jump in, stay down for twenty minutes, follow the compass to a certain point, and that's where they would pick me up. *Good luck.* And that's where this chapter began.

Somehow I survived that gruesome experience. And while learning to dive may not be on any textbook list of adversities or major stress factors, it was a giant obstacle for me to overcome. At several points I thought I was going to die, and it required me to face my greatest fears. Stress is different for everyone based on their unique situation. The person who has swum in the ocean would probably not comprehend why this story was a challenge and so scary for me. Likewise, if someone was afraid of public speaking, I may not relate to that fear since I've always loved the opportunity to speak to a group. The bigger the audience, the better. Our fears, phobias, and levels of what *we think* we cannot handle are all different.

The rewards of my challenging, freezing January dive tests were great. In addition to realizing I was ready to conquer other fears and the newfound courage to achieve higher goals, there were other benefits ahead. The next week, I was in Cozumel, Mexico, just a few days after obtaining my Professional Association of Diving Instructors (PADI) dive certification license. It was unbelievably amazing! The Caribbean water was warm, and swimming with the most beautiful tropical fish was breathtaking. The word *swimming* is not actually appropriate since no skills were required. The dives were referred to as *drift dives*, which meant we were dropped off at one point in the ocean. Then after going to our designated depth (usually thirty-to-sixty feet), the current of the water would gently move us along until our divemaster would gesture that it was time to go back up to the fifteen-feet point. We were to then wait there until it was time to surface back to get on the boat. Each time I came up, I was super excited to go back down and explore more. It could not have been more beautiful or peaceful. We got to do this every day while we were there, and there were no bad dives.

One day an experienced diver friend asked the captain if he would take us out further so that we could dive in the caves. He specifically requested a dive at a place called *the Devil's Throat*. The Spanish translation is "La Garganta del Diablo." This was an underwater cave formation near Cozumel, Mexico, at Punta Sur. It starts at approximately eighty feet and then proceeds to go down to about one hundred fifty feet. We had several divers in our boat, and three of them chose not to do this dive, as it was apparently a bit dangerous. I now realize that only the more experienced divers should attempt to dive through a series of narrow tunnels dropping through the red, coral reef structures. I also now realize it would be very scary for anyone with claustrophobia. Each diver was given a choice of whether they wanted to participate in this potentially risky dive.

I was immediately ready to go! *Let's do this!* Since I was the least experienced diver with less than one week of experience compared to the many years or even decades of diving for the rest of the group, I had been assigned to the divemaster himself as my dive partner. He had become my fearless leader, so I decided I could do this if he was with me. So we jumped out of the boat and proceeded to manipulate the narrow tunnels. The hardest part was keeping our oxygen (O_2) tanks and associated hoses from touching the reef through these confined spaces. I thought I remembered them saying at one point we were below the two hundred feet point, but now I think that was wrong, as our O_2 would have run out. But we made it back up, and though our O_2 was low, all was well.

Another key point that I learned from diving, especially where O_2 needs to be cautiously preserved, is slow breathing techniques.

During the early classroom phase, I learned how each diver must resist the urge to breathe rapidly, as they might do in a panic situation. That would use up too much of your limited oxygen in too short of a time period. Instead, you must consciously force yourself to breathe very slowly to conserve as much oxygen as possible. I developed this skill early on. If I learned nothing else, I could at least be a good slow breather! This trait has proven to be useful in other life situations where I'm faced with overwhelming stress. My body wants to go into the pure panic mode, but instead I resort to the slow and steady breathing mode. It's remarkable how this can slow the heart rate and calm the mind.

The physical actions demanded more than I thought was possible, but rising to the mental challenges to override fears and doubts was even greater.

This diving experience helped me to build resilience in many ways. The physical actions demanded more than I thought was possible, but rising to the mental challenges to override fears and doubts was even greater. I feel stronger on both levels because of those challenges.

Practice slow and steady breathing to override stress and panic in times of fear or anxiety. For example, breathe in for a slow count of five seconds. Hold your breath for another five seconds; then slowly breathe out for five seconds. Keep doing this for several minutes to calm your racing heartbeat and relax the tension in your body as you also stop the anxiety and panic that is often the result of stress.

Chapter 7

JOB CHANGES AND LOSSES

S INCE I'VE HELD MANY CORPORATE OPERATIONAL POSITIONS, YOU would think I can logically understand that acquisitions and mergers will happen, and we should not take them personally. But my own personal issues are that I have given each of my positions one hundred fifty percent effort and have often placed my job as a much higher priority than I should have allowed. Technically there should be no more than one hundred percent, right? In my case, since my mission was always to develop new projects, achieve budget, and fill every waking moment with initiatives for what I felt would be good for the company, I now realize these actions were far beyond my one hundred percent. I have heard that men more than women find their identity in their career roles, which may be their title. However, I fit in that category as well, where I have most often found my identity and purpose in my career.

I've also held many volunteer roles in the community and in my professional organizations. These range from being on committees and boards to working with caregiver organizations, where I volunteer to teach or work as a care partner to give caregivers a little time for themselves. I even have a separate "church volunteer resume." A senior pastor once looked at it and said, "Well, it looks like you've held every church position except senior pastor over the last twenty-five years!" My point is that, for most of my life, I was unable to just show up and be present. I immediately had to volunteer to fill a needed role. That also meant that I was working in those capacities for an additional thirty-to-forty hours a week in addition to my job that has always held at least sixty-to-seventy hours of my time on Monday through Friday.

Before I describe my experiences with job loss, let me share the types of positions I've held. My first job out of graduate school was as a speech language pathologist in a nursing home. But that was back when contract therapy companies were first getting contracts to provide therapy in nursing homes. So the market was rapidly growing. Then, the day I finished my nine-month clinical fellowship and completed the paperwork with my clinical fellowship supervisor, I was suddenly put into a new role. Valerie Quinter was my supervisor, and she was also the district manager for West TN. Because I had been volunteering to help her with the quality assurance process for all our district's claims at the end of every month, she decided I was the one to replace her in her current role, since the company was sending her to manage operations in Florida. She told me she had two weeks to teach me everything about this new role, and then she would be on vacation before her ultimate move to Florida. That was the quick conversation that initiated my twenty-five years of rehab operations, beginning with Pro-Rehab then with other corporate operational roles.

As I initially experienced several corporate acquisitions, things were still fine, and I was always a part of the package that was sold. In fact, I once had a friend in Austin who asked me, "Aren't you ever afraid of losing your job in this high-risk health care operations job?" I immediately responded, "Of course not! I'm a great asset to the company, and when things change, I always land on my feet!" Now I realize that was a very naïve thing to say because no one is indispensable. Several years after that, I worked as a vice president for the Texas region, for a therapy company out of Alabama, and

I received an unexpected call from my boss, the president of the company. He had decided to sell his company to a large nursing home chain based in Phoenix. Despite the fact that I had exceeded all his set goals for my Texas territory, the new company would decide my future. That's when I learned that companies with their own vice presidents often do not want to inherit or employ the vice presidents for those companies that they have acquired. It's just extra cost. Therefore, not only did I suddenly have no job, but the company to whom he sold his business had filed Chapter 13, so they didn't have to pay my contract's severance package.

I could not even comprehend being unemployed. It was 1999, the year that our entire Medicare system changed for therapy reimbursement. Companies were laying off therapy staff or closing their doors, unable to figure out how to stay in business. To complicate matters, I was recently divorced with a four-year-old daughter and had just sold my house and put all my savings into building a large custom home. We had just moved into an apartment while the house was being built. Overnight, it was as if I had lost everything.

A job loss is complex. People may first think of the lost income, but there's also a loss of identity. There are many unknowns about what the future may or may not hold. There are pitiful looks and questions from your friends in the community and at church and from prior colleagues. I remember sitting at my desk for eight hours each day, applying for every possible job that existed. On good days, I felt as though I could do a stand-up comedy act by describing the types of jobs to which I had applied that day. Since most positions like my own had been deleted with the Medicare changes, I applied for any type of director position, ranging from managing a restaurant to positions that included words I didn't even comprehend. Then things seemed to worsen. I broke my leg while playing football at a church single adult retreat and could only get around on crutches. I lived in a second-floor apartment with no elevator.

My unemployment lasted for more than five months before I took a position for a HealthSouth hospital to manage their therapy operations. I really enjoyed that position until my senior operations colleagues began to tell me something was happening with the company, but none of us knew the details, and no one could figure it out. Soon after that, we all left our jobs there, except for the director of nursing. By this time, I had met my future husband, which was great! He was the one who convinced me to leave HealthSouth based on what I told him. He also explained that I needed the time at home, since we had just learned that my father, who lived five hours away in Louisiana, had pancreatic cancer, and my daughter was starting kindergarten and needed my time in the evenings to support this big change in her life.

After a few more months, I accepted a position as practice administrator for a large nephrology office. That was very different than anything I had ever done. I learned a lot, including accurate accounting systems, for which I hired an accountant to teach me and to complete monthly audits on my work. Until then, they had outsourced their accounts payable, and I decided they were being robbed by the outsourced company who was covering the details with reports that were so complex, no one at the office could read them. So I took all accounting functions in-house and worked to improve accuracy and efficiency. The only problem with that job was the salary, which was a third of what I was used to making. That was a big issue as the cost of living was much higher in Austin.

Eventually I accepted another job, which required us to move to Dallas but would allow me to be back in my corporate therapy world. It required traveling around the country about eighty percent of the time, and by then I had a five-month-old son. My husband said the words I feared when he cautioned, "Our son will not even know who you are." It was also a bad fit for my skills. I was good at administrative therapy operations that included working closely with nursing home administrators, budgets, and employee management, but they needed me to write clinical manuals. At that time, I had not worked in a hands-on clinical role for many years.

Finally I was hired to be a regional director for a nationwide therapy company. My territory quickly grew from four to twenty-five nursing homes. I was back in my happy world, doing what I did best. I had two hundred fifty employees, was able to provide collaborative friendships with nursing home leaders, was able to teach regulatory changes, and succeeded with all set budgets and profitability reports.

I also loved providing recognition of the great therapy teams and taught leadership skills to all the directors.

Then my husband's company was sold, and it was his turn to be laid off. He likewise received one hundred percent of his identity from work, where he was a sales engineer and a project manager and was well respected in his switchgear/power field. But for some reason he couldn't get another job in the Dallas area where we lived.

He was later offered a position in South Louisiana, just forty-five minutes from my hometown. I decided to resign from my regional operational position with a sixty-day notice and to look for a speech language pathologist (SLP) staff position in a nursing home in that area. I knew that an SLP in a rural area would have the highest hourly rate, and I could make almost the same amount of money for much fewer hours/week. Keep in mind that as a regional director in Dallas, I rarely worked less than eighty hours/week to stay on top of all issues. SLPs usually work thirty-five-to-forty hours/week and make the same amount of money. What a big difference. I needed to spend more time with my children who, at that time, were four and twelve. That was a huge learning experience for me!

I then provided speech therapy services to three rural Louisiana nursing homes. This meant I forced myself to study nonstop every night to catch up on the latest evidence-based practice clinical techniques. I was good at documentation, since I had taught employees how to write skilled documentation for the last twenty years. But I had to get better at everything else, including treating swallowing problems and cognition and language deficits for people with strokes, progressive and degenerative diseases, and any other condition causing such declines in function. I also had to quickly build a library of resources to do all of that. I made it work and very much liked being on a clinical team again with the physical therapy (PT) and occupational therapy (OT) staff, working closely with nurses, dietary managers, social workers, and the entire staff of each home. I continued to teach conferences on the weekend, so this interprofessional experience was an asset for me to reference such new skills in my courses.

I then moved into a compliance and education role for that same company, which was a great fit for me as well. By that time, I was back on top of the game from a clinical standpoint. I had a good grasp on the assessments and treatments by all therapy disciplines, so I could work in this role to create resources for them and to do anything my senior vice president or her team needed. I was back again in my eighty-hour workweek, but I loved it!

My husband was successful in his role, so they transferred us back to Texas for him to be their project manager/switchgear specialist from their corporate headquarters. I continued to work in my compliance/education role until I seemed to hit a burnout point. I even became very ill with pyelonephritis and sepsis and was hospitalized in the ICU for several days. Eventually I resigned and worked as an SLP in the local nursing home while looking for my next career move.

From there, I went to Windsor Rehab in an education role. This was an in-house therapy company for a group of Texas nursing homes. That was a great job as well, as I was able to work with a new colleague, Greg Pfahles, who was a critical care cardiac nurse with a great deal of knowledge and expertise about our geriatric and cardiac residents. Together we developed many courses and taught them in hospitals and nursing homes across Texas. This experience escalated my growing interest in the field of pharmacy, including the adverse effects of drug-drug interactions in older people. I was fortunate to stay there for over two years before it was time to move on.

I was recruited by a prior colleague to be an education specialist for another nationwide company, Select Rehabilitation. In that role, I had the privilege of developing and recording courses for our internal university system and was also sent around the country to different states' LeadingAge conferences and to various states' health care association conferences. I was able to create education resources for many of the VPs' regions in the company to research and provide training on their requested health care topics.

Then something devastating happened—completely unexpected and challenging on every level. The pandemic began in mid-February 2020, and in April I received the call that I was being furloughed. I was told it would hopefully be very short, so I would just need to send my company laptop back but keep the printer for when I could resume my job at some point, though they did not know when. My email and phone would be turned off at the end of the day. Since my job was my entire life, I used only that one email and that one phone number. I quickly created an email account and forwarded different personal/business accounts to the new email address, but it wasn't enough. I felt an overwhelming sense of paralyzing panic and couldn't even think of what to do next. Since the company had started to directly pay my phone bill, they also now owned that number and phone. So I had to go get another phone (and phone number), which subsequently made me lose all my contacts and all options to reach anyone I knew. It was a very traumatic experience. I now know to always keep a personal phone and a personal email, but back then it was convenient to only check one email account, and since I worked twelve hours a day, I didn't think I had time to also check another account. Another naïve decision. To make matters worse, my husband had received a similar call two weeks before, only they let him keep his insurance to cover our family. They also gave him a return date for August and did not leave him guessing.

Three months after my furlough began, my husband and I had driven to my hometown to attend the funeral of my dear friend's father, Edward Goins. We lost cell service for most of the drive through Louisiana, but when we arrived, I had a short period of service and checked my new personal email account. I saw a short, generic email that said something like,

> *Dear employee, since you have been furloughed for 3 months now, we are now terminating your contract.*

Then they gave some kind of instructions about how to send their printer back.

At that point I went into full panic attack. *What? What about resuming my role?* I had not even considered looking for another job since I was overly committed and beyond loyal to my own company. The worst part about all of that very bad experience was that the same corporate team who I had called my friends sent me a *generic* letter without even a personal call. I experienced stages of shock and denial well before the anger kicked in. I chose not to tell anyone for a very long time because I didn't want the company to look bad. It was probably a full two years later that I referenced this loss on a Facebook post when a photo came up from one month before, where I had received a big award. That was before everything changed and I lost my job.

I can end this story here by saying it was much more devastating than it should have been. I should say, "It was just a job," but it was my fault for making it so much more and for giving too much of myself to a company. I thought I was secure by being in education and not operations. I thought if I produced twice as many webinars as others on my team and agreed to travel to teach in more states for them that I would be appreciated.

Since then, I've had to really think about my priorities and my overcommitments to an employer and admit my mistakes in thinking otherwise. That employer was doing what they needed to do. They were laying off hundreds of people at the same moment, so they had no time for calls. I later read that this company had chosen to cut all possible costs at that time to be able to acquire an even larger company, which was ironically the one that had acquired my company back in 1999. It's strange how small our corporate therapy world really is.

All is well now. I started my own LLC, teaching webinars for three-to-four different companies, working three days/week for a rural nursing home as well as for a clinic, and seeing home health patients and supervising at another nursing home. For the next three years, I had seven employers from whom I pieced together an income. Now I'm back to a happy place and am working for what used to be Windsor Rehab—now they are Regency IHS Therapy Management. I now work with the best corporate and regional team ever and can truly say that I am very grateful!

Breathe, move forward, focus on a new opportunity, and stop grieving the loss of what just happened.

All of these job losses and transitions were not planned. I would have much rather had the opportunity to work for one employer, stay loyal to them, and retire there after fifty years. But that is not realistic. Very few people get to do that anymore.

I will say that my job changes have required a great deal of resilience. Each end of a job felt like a death in some way. And then there's a need to breathe, move forward, focus on a new opportunity, and stop grieving the loss of what just happened. The period between leaving one position and starting another is sometimes like a black hole, full of questions with no answers. There's a lot of second-guessing yourself. Why?

My experience with developing resilience in this context included a phrase that my friend Kim Williams told me after my 1999 job loss. We were sitting in choir practice in Austin, Texas. At the time, I was divorced, had a broken leg, had a four-year-old daughter to take care of, and had no job or income. She asked me, "How are you doing?" Of course I replied, "I'm good. Somehow it will all work out OK." She replied, "Yes, God has me on a need-to-know basis too."

That became my mantra. God has everything worked out for my future! He will always make a way when there seems to be no way. He has given me multiple talents, and He will find a place for me to use them. He just has me on a "need-to-know" basis while He works out the final details and prepares me for the next steps.

My mindset changed when I reflected on everything I learned in each of the positions I've held—things I would have otherwise never known or learned. Therefore, I choose to be grateful for every opportunity and for every transition, even for those that abruptly ended.

I will admit that I would very much like to stay in my current position and company for another ten years and to apply all that I've learned. I do hope that will be the case! But if that's not possible, everything will still be OK.

Focus on lessons learned through each unexpected challenge. Remind yourself that God has you on a "need-to-know" basis. He has everything under control and will walk you through this trial, making sure you see victory on the other side.

Chapter 8

MOVING FORWARD
AFTER DIVORCE

I N THE BLISSFULLY EXCITING MOMENTS OF GETTING MARRIED, I would think that not many consider the risks and potential for divorce. Even though statistics say that forty-to-fifty percent of marriages end in divorce, most of us think that will not happen to us.[17] This is especially true for those of us who think of best-case scenarios and who focus more on the positive. We perceive marriage as living through all the stages of life with our best friend and soulmate, having children, and growing old together. Then at some point reality hits, and once we are in our married life, we realize that marriage can be the greatest challenge we've ever experienced. Such is often the case when the two people involved have different perspectives on what is important to them and what is not. And even when they may initially be focused on the same

---

17. "Divorce Rate in America: 48 Divorce Statistics," CDC/National Center for Health Statistics, updated 2023, www.census.gov/library/visualizations/interactive/marriage-divorce-rates-by-state-2011-2021.html.

things, priorities may change, and their unique plans may take them on completely different paths in opposite directions. There are so many factors involved, and each couple has their own challenges.

In my case, I was a workaholic, leading my region for a national organization. I was very driven to achieve work goals and to support all my employees to be their best so that we could then be the best region with the highest achievements in the company. I lived and breathed for work. I was also a leader in many areas of my church, including teaching Sunday school and children's musicals; singing with the church worship team, which required several hours a week of rehearsals and learning solos every week; and working as a youth leader with a one-hundred-plus member youth group. There was no down time in my life. No relaxation. No vacations. I got minimal sleep and was extremely goal-oriented to achieve more. I considered myself a highly disciplined person, which I perceived as a good thing. But after a few years of this, I recognized that I had no fun in my life. Nothing to look forward to. I decided I was boring and was missing out on what should bring joy to my life.

One of the guys in the college career class that I taught constantly volunteered to help me with the youth newsletter and other projects. Let's just call him John. He was nineteen, and I was twenty-five. When my running partner moved away, this guy would show up to run with me. He would make me laugh and constantly work to get my attention. One Saturday afternoon, when I was in the midst of a twelve-hour commitment to documentation analyses of all month-end paperwork, he showed up at my apartment and convinced me to go with him for a twenty-minute motorcycle ride because I "needed a break." I rarely took a break. *What's a break?* But somehow he convinced me, and I was shocked at how much fun I could have in that short period of time. I laughed and felt exhilarated!

I returned to work until 11:30 p.m. Then I jumped in the car and raced to take my completed work packet to the airport FedEx office by their midnight deadline. I then returned to my apartment for my late-night five-mile run through the Memphis suburb of Bartlett. That night I thought about the fact that maybe I should have more fun in my life. But it was a risk, and I didn't know how to work it in with all my other responsibilities.

After several months with "fun" John in my life, trying to make me laugh and constantly volunteering to help me with my various projects, we actually went on a few dates. It just kind of evolved. Then I bought a house and continued to grow in my career, including adding another state to my territory. John convinced me to buy a Mazda Miata because it was a fun car. I already had a cool, sporty SAAB, but the Miata was more fun. He taught me to drive a five-speed on a rental car; then I bought the little red sports car. That was definitely a fun car to drive! I put the top down and drove it for over one hundred thousand miles over the next two years—all over Arkansas, Tennessee, and Texas. Life was getting better!

Then the next chapter began. On a whim, John convinced me to marry him. He was twenty, and I was twenty-six. I convinced myself that he would be the antidote to my overly disciplined life. Within a week of that conversation, we went to the courthouse and got married. I honestly thought it would be great, but there was so much more to this complicated picture. I'll spare the details, as this book is not about blaming others. But I learned that John was an alcoholic, with many misperceptions about marriage and an uncontrollable urge to drink. His alcoholism and behavior ultimately led to an abusive environment and financial harm. Our marriage was not the *fun* life I had anticipated.

For several years I decided I had made a commitment to John, and this would just have to be the rest of my life. But I felt no love. Surprisingly, after three years, we started talking about having a baby. I decided, perhaps in desperation, that this was a great idea because a baby would bring me the love I needed! I wanted a little girl. So about seven months after I turned thirty, we had a precious little girl, Alexandra Laycie. I was in love with my amazing daughter.

We worked hard to be a sweet little family, but John was still an alcoholic, and our marriage and home continued to decline. Over time and through many difficult situations, I realized that I could not leave our daughter in his care anymore while I was at work. So I enrolled her in a daycare.

My little Alex was an early talker. She participated in a University of Texas language development study where they tracked her communication skills at twelve months, fourteen months, and eighteen months. They tracked language skills for many babies born the same week in Austin, Texas, to compare with the language development of children born the same week in Chile. I remember at eighteen months her language sample included her saying, "After this we're going to the grocery store, then the bank, then to Kinkos!" She loved going with me on all my errands. Talking with her was like communicating with a very tiny little adult.

When she was two-and-a-half years old, one day she asked me why her daddy was screaming at me again. Something clicked in my brain, and the harsh reality hit me. I realized I had to end my marriage. I could not allow my daughter to grow up in such a dysfunctional environment. I had developed ways to cope with the devolving situation, but now I realized my coping mechanisms were not protecting my little girl from the chaos and turmoil of our home. I prayed much about what to do—what God, my Abba Father's, will was for my life and my marriage. He probably grieved on my behalf when I married, knowing what was to come. Life was very hard. None of my choices seemed to be the right ones. But ultimately I decided I had to leave my dysfunctional and verbally abusive marriage for my daughter's sake and my own sanity.

John and I then had the much-needed conversation and agreed to get a divorce. Surprisingly we were both relieved, as it had never really worked between us. We agreed to all terms and conditions before calling the attorney to keep the costs low. John agreed not to take half the house, since I had paid for all the bills, and I agreed to pay off all the high credit card bills he had run up without my knowledge.

Even though this divorce was needed and would allow us both to move on in our completely different desired directions, it was hard. I felt like a failure. This was the first thing I had ever pursued that was a complete disaster. But I had a daughter, and I needed to move forward with life and create the most positive, loving, and nurturing home possible for her. There were still continued struggles with John's visitation and planned weekends with our daughter. Alcoholism makes everything unpredictable, difficult, and sometimes scary.

Even so, some weekends were great, and John would plan fun weekends with our daughter—including time with his best friend's family, who also had a child, and they could do family-friendly things together. But other weekends were not so nice. I never knew what to expect when I dropped her off. Would John be dazed and confused, asleep on the couch, or smiling and ready to go? Sometimes I had to just turn around and take my daughter home and make new plans for us for the weekend.

Before continuing with this discussion of resiliency after divorce, I should add that a few years after our divorce, John moved on to get help. His mom and supportive family convinced him to move back home, and while there in a supportive environment, he stopped drinking, got a job, and became the great guy he was meant to be. Our daughter, Alex, was even able to go live with him while getting her associate's degree.

I'm glad to say things are much better now. I do not blame him. John always wanted to be a great dad. But alcoholism is a real disease that can ruin a person and their relationships.

Apparently divorce represents the death of the most significant of relationships. This then triggers major adjustments and changes to a person's identity in every part of their life.

Looking back, I should have known better the risk of our marriage not working out. But for several months after our divorce, I could only think about my failure in life. Divorce is often listed as the second-most stressful life event, preceded only by the death of a spouse. Apparently divorce represents the death of the most significant of relationships. This then triggers major adjustments and changes to a person's identity in every part of their life.

When I got a divorce, I was a vice president of a therapy company. I did not tell anyone at work, including my boss. He depended on me to run a third of his company, and I did not want him to even remotely wonder if my emotional status might affect my leadership and management decisions. So once again, I compartmentalized my emotions and worked full speed ahead to ensure all responsibilities were taken care of, stopping to reflect on my personal failures only on the weekends or in early mornings when my daughter was asleep.

I finally told both bosses when they came to Austin to visit me. They were physical therapists and college roommates who had started a company and now ran it together as the president and the chief operating officer. My divorce had been final for six months, so while sitting at dinner at the Oasis one night, a favorite restaurant near my home on the lake, I told them, "First, I need you both to know that I've got everything under control, and my region is doing very well. Second, I want to now share that I got a divorce six months ago." They were in shock and had no idea.

Immediately following my separation and John leaving my home, my strategy for managing this overwhelming stress and anger with myself for this life failure was to compulsively clean and reorganize every spot in my house. I prayed a lot, ran as many miles as I could every day, and focused my mind on being the best mother possible and assuring all goals for my regional territory were met. I also left the church where I had served as a college career teacher, a worship leader, and a women's group leader. I had many friends there, but if there was any chance for John to be a part of a church, even if through periodic attendance, it would be there. He loved the pastor, Rex Johnson, and there was a chance he could seek help there. But we couldn't go to the same church.

I moved to another great and larger church in Austin, now known as the Promiseland. For the first few weeks, I sat in the balcony and absorbed all the music and sermons and received all the encouragement I needed. I had a very good friend there, Monique Chase, who had previously been a part of my other church. She encouraged me to join the one-hundred-plus-member choir, and I did. At first I didn't know anyone, and it was a bit intimidating.

But soon I had several new best friends there, and they became a big part of this new chapter of my life.

My journey to resiliency following divorce started with building what I now know as physical resilience. This included the actions of cleaning and organizing my home, running, and other forms of physical exercise. These actions effectively helped me manage and control my anxiety and improve my focus on all existing and future priorities.

I now see this, but at that point I had no idea what resiliency was. I sought mental resilience through prayer, music, singing, and spending time with new friends. I joined a new young adult group, which offered fun events for people my age. I visualized my positive future and made myself focus on what I had

> **Cleaning and organizing my home, running, and other forms of physical exercise. . . . effectively helped me manage and control my anxiety and improve my focus on all existing and future priorities.**

accomplished in other areas of my life so I could gradually stop thinking about my recent failure. My emotional resilience at that point had been strengthened by the foundation of physical and mental resiliency. I now know that these other resiliency forms allowed me to tame my amygdala to control emotions and anxiety.

Divorce affects people in many ways. Initially there will likely be stages of grief, much like after a death. This often includes denial, shock, and despair, which might also include tears, anger, and resentment. Simultaneously the person may also experience different levels of financial loss and increased debt, which adds to their lack of stability. Depending on the circumstances, the person may feel a decrease in self-esteem and may not feel *good enough*, thinking of their own personal failure. This could lead to a lower quality of life, ongoing emotional problems, depression, and a general decrease in life function.

Many people in my life have shared their own personal experience with divorce. Some exhibit deep levels of pain and anger, depending on the circumstances. Most share their accounts of financial loss, as assets are often divided. Some are still angry many years later after their spouse surprised them with divorce papers. I've heard many stories of one parent pitting their children against the other parent, saying he or she is horribly in the wrong. There are so many negative outcomes from some divorces. In such cases, recovery takes much longer, and in every case, counseling would be very helpful. Moving forward requires forgiveness, agreeing to disagree, and shifting one's focus and daily mindset on a positive future for all.

Divorce can also result in a new chapter of life. Despite the initial pain, it can lead us to fervently seek God's direction. Following these prayers, God often directs us to remove the obstacles in our lives that are preventing us from accomplishing the goals He has for us. With these distractions out of the way, He can open our eyes to new opportunities. Each new day brings fresh mercy and a renewed hope for the future. Eventually the resiliency following divorce is the foundation for the needed freedom to move beyond the negative emotions and to experience God's direction for more positive, personal growth.

Seek new opportunities every day to build resilience following a broken relationship. Consider adding more daily physical activity to transform your brain and thought patterns. Then add prayer, music, and positive experiences with friends to bring mental and emotional resilience. Maintain such daily activities, and you will eventually feel a greater resiliency and strength.

Chapter 9

THE GOOD, BAD, AND UGLY EFFECTS OF STRESS

ONE OF THE MANY TOPICS I'VE RESEARCHED AND TAUGHT ABOUT is stress management. To begin, there are different types of *stress*. When most of us think about stress we think about the bad kind, what we refer to as *distress*. Yet there are other types of good stress that we call *eustress*—that elated feeling when you win the lottery or something amazing has just happened. I believe that I feel a type of eustress when I accomplish things. Or when I get to teach to a large audience. What a thrill that is for me to see their positive responses and to hear them later tell me how much they learned. Yay!

There is significant research on the subject of stress that shows that a moderate amount of the right kind of stress can actually help people to be happier and more productive at work. Though this is cited in current research, there's an older model dating back to 1908 called the "Yerkes-Dodson Law" that explains how either too much or too little stress can affect a person's job performance, satisfaction, and health.[18,19]

Yerkes - Dodson Law: Optimal Stress Level

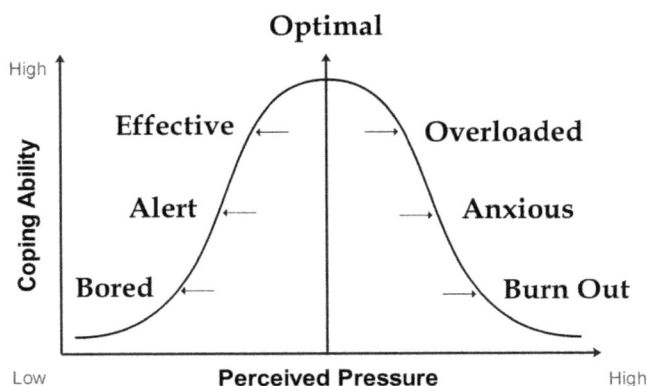

Figure 1. Yerkes-Dodson Law: Too much/little = stress

Since then, much research has been published on how even a little stress can energize a person to be more proactive and productive in their work. It then serves to motivate rather than debilitate their abilities. Dr. Wendy Suzuki, a neuroscientist at New York University, and Peter Vitaliano, a professor of psychiatry and behavioral sciences at the University of Washington School of Medicine, suggest that we should endorse stress as a challenge rather than a problem, which will then help us to improve our work quality and our well-being.[20]

18. Charlotte Nickerson, "The Yerkes-Dodson Law of Arousal and Performance," Simply Psychology (November 9, 2023), https://www.simplypsychology.org/what-is-the-yerkes-dodson-law.html.

19. Robert M. Yerkes and John D. Dodson, "The Relation of Strength of Stimulus to Rapidity of Habit Formation," *Journal of Comparative Neurology & Psychology* 18 (1908): 459–482, https://doi.org/10.1002/cne.920180503.

20. Wendy Suzuki with Billie Fitzpatrick, *Good Anxiety: Harnessing the Power of the Most Misunderstood Emotion* (NY: Atria Books, 2022).

Let's now dive into the lesser-known sources of debility that stem from underlying stress. The human body is fearfully and wonderfully made (Psalm 139:14), which includes remarkable and complex systems that function to protect us and to allow complicated daily functions and executive brain functions in order to think, plan, and respond to threats. However, unmanaged stress can have detrimental effects on a person's body.

> **We should endorse stress as a challenge rather than a problem, which will then help us to improve our work quality and our well-being.**

When a person perceives a stressful situation, whether it is a real threat or a potential fear or threat, his or her body will respond with a physiological response called the *conserved transcriptional response to adversity* (CTRA).[21] You will know this as the "fight or flight" response. With this stress point triggered, the body responds by prompting the hypothalamus to tell the adrenal glands to release stress hormones, such as adrenaline and cortisol. These hormones increase the heartbeat and send blood rushing to the areas needed for emergencies, such as the muscles, heart, and other important organs. But in order for the body to ramp up those functions, other body systems and mechanisms must decrease, such as the immune system. The body will also increase pro-inflammatory genes and decrease downregulated expressions of Type I interferons and antibody-related genes. That means that inflammation is increased, which may lead to other disease processes if the stress is ongoing or chronic.[22]

A very interesting fact about this CTRA, or fight or flight response, is the difference in how human beings and animals perceive it. An animal's body responds in much the same way as a

21. Steven W. Cole, "The Conserved Transcriptional Response to Adversity," *Current Opinion in Behavioral Sciences* 28 (2019): 31–37, https://doi.org/10.1016/j.cobeha.2019.01.008.

22. Michalina Frankowska and Magdalena Błażek, "Positive Affect, Well-Being and the Human Conserved Transcriptional Response to Adversity: A Descriptive Review," *European Journal of Translational and Clinical Medicine* 5, no. 2 (October 5, 2022), DOI: 10.31373/ejtcm/152870.

human, except they will only develop this response when faced with an actual threat or danger. The body will ramp up these immediate functions to run or fight; then, when they are safe again, their body will begin to return to normal levels. Their immunity will be restored, and inflammatory factors will decrease. That process takes several hours to be restored, and then they are back to their restored levels of calm and peace. Humans, however, can trigger this response by just thinking about a perceived threat even though the threat has not yet happened. This leads to an ongoing release of cortisol and adrenaline. But the fight or flight response was meant to sense harm and protect us in that moment, so it should technically only last for a short time. During that time, in order for us to feel the increase in our senses (such as blood pumping faster and a higher heart rate), other systems need to decrease (such as our immune system). But if there is no actual immediate danger, and we allow ourselves to continue to dwell on the "what if" worst-case scenarios, we then remain in that state. What should have been a short-term reaction to survive becomes a prolonged state of mind.[23]

For example, someone could think, *What if I lose my job? What if he/she leaves me? What if I lose my child? What if. . . ?* In these cases, a person could live in a chronic state of decreased immunity and increased inflammation without ever allowing their bodies to return to normal levels of function. The short-term effects of this ongoing stress may include,

- cardiovascular and respiratory system issues, beginning with increased blood pressure and respiration rates
- headaches
- back and shoulder pain triggered by tightened muscles
- increased glucose production
- heartburn and other gastrointestinal issues
- decreased testosterone
- increased menopause symptoms and other hormonal problems

23. Roger Landry, *Live Long, Die Short: A Guide to Authentic Health and Successful Aging* (Austin, TX: Greenleaf Book Group, 2014).

- poor sleep quality
- lower immunity or low resistance to disease
- slower wound healing

. . . (to name a few). The long-term effects may include higher levels of chronic conditions, such as diabetes, arthritis, ulcers, and anemia, as well as many other potential chronic disease factors. This could then lead to more prescription medications, more potential negative effects of polypharmacy, and a lower quality of life and health, leading to an earlier death. Such physiological responses to stress can worsen over time, so the longer we remain in a state of stress, the greater the impact to the body.[24]

The following are a few examples of the stages of stress:

- *Short-term stress:* Anticipation of adversity, increased sensitivity to pain, social anxiety

- *Mid-term stress:* Disrupted sleep, chronic pain, depressed mood, social withdrawal

- *Long-term stress:* Susceptibility to infection, inflammatory diseases (e.g., diabetes, arthritis, asthma, heart disease, Alzheimer's disease, cancer), accelerated aging, early death[25]

Given all the facts and what we know about how stress can further debilitate the body, we can then understand how important it is for us to focus on points of resilience. Stress management strategies can be very effective to stop the ongoing release of stress hormones that leads to such a decline. It is absolutely possible to get to the point where we are not living in fear and worrying about the "what if" situations.

Joyce Sunada's quote sums up the need for prioritizing our plans to decrease debilitating stress: "Make time for your wellness,

24. Eunsoo Won and Yong-Ku Kim, "Neuroinflammation-Associated Alterations of the Brain as Potential Neural Biomarkers in Anxiety Disorders," *International Journal of Molecular Sciences* 21, no. 18 (September 7, 2020): 6,546. doi: 10.3390/ijms21186546.

25. Rebecca L. Acabchuk, Jayesh Kamath, John D. Salamone, and Blair T. Johnson, "Stress and Chronic Illness: The Inflammatory Pathway," *Social Science & Medicine* 185 (July 2017): 166–170, doi: 10.1016/j.socscimed.2017.04.039.

or you will be forced to take time for your illness." So at this point, we can now see the importance of seeking resilience. Details of strategies to achieve this goal will be covered later.

Before moving on, here's another story about a friend who experienced her own challenges and how she sought resilience to move forward.

KIMBERLY

Kimberly is a great mom of two great sons and the wife of a successful husband and high school coach. She's adorable and loved by many, including the many children she has helped in her role as a speech language pathologist. She helps students who cannot communicate their wants and needs to find a way to interact in their environments.

One day, she had a seemingly routine hysterectomy that altered her entire life. The surgeon stapled a nerve during the procedure, which then resulted in her having to learn to live with chronic pain for the rest of her life. Kimberly shared, "I initially couldn't walk without excruciating pain. I could not find medical professionals in my town with knowledge of what was happening to me [so they could] help. I couldn't take the pain pills they gave me because I couldn't function, so I began a quest to find an alternate way to live."

In the beginning, the pain was so intense Kimberly couldn't imagine ever having a normal life again. She was able to find one physical therapist in her entire northern Louisiana city that kept her from losing hope. Every other health professional gave her none. Finally, she found a team of doctors in Houston, which included a urologist, a gynecologist, a pelvic nerve specialist, and an osteopathic doctor. She was then referred to a pelvic PT in Lake Charles, LA. It was these professionals who changed her life and gave her new hope. The daily pain and not being able to function or interact with her kids and husband took a toll on everyone.

Kimberly sought to find strength from all sources. She shared that her husband was incredible throughout the entire experience.

He tried to make every journey to Houston an adventure. She joined online Bible studies to find hope and redirection. She would leave her family to live in a hotel in Lake Charles for periods of time to get the PT treatments she needed, but she found those weeks to be very lonely. She wore the prayer shawl her church gave her, and it helped her to get through the nights.

After five years, Kimberly was able to stop the extreme travel and begin managing the pain with the tools she had been given. She joined a Facebook group that included other people who also had similar experiences with this unique medical diagnosis. She found the group to be very helpful, and she began to feel that she was giving hope to others as well.

Recently she has new options in her own city that include a physical therapist who specializes in pelvic disorders. She was able to work with this PT to get back on track with updated strategies for pain management.

Kimberly shared how she also found other things to be helpful that she thought might seem minor or silly to others. For example, she set her phone ringtone to be Mandisa's "Overcomer" song. She also reminded herself how blessed she is to be able to walk and to lift a gallon of milk again, though she still needs to be careful with any lifting.

As she shared her story, Kimberly concluded with her thoughts on hope for others:

> It took so many years, it would be easy to give up. But don't; keep trying. Keep searching for the things that will touch you, speak to you, and change you. It's that gift of hope as we struggle through pain that you must keep in your sight. Make it your ringtone, write yourself notes in the mirror, increase your self-talk of positive words. Those around me may not have said the right things or prescribed the right things, but staying open to what was around me let me pull from those things what helped me the most when I was able to finally help myself.

Each person's story is real, and each person has sought and found their resilience in different ways. We are all unique in our challenges and abilities, but we must all ultimately find our way to move forward—where we seek our path to physical, spiritual, and emotional resilience. This is an active process that requires focus on a plan. Without a plan, we succumb to perpetual residence in a place of fear, debility, and a stagnancy, which then leads to further loss.

Encourage yourself by focusing on what you can do rather than on what you can no longer do. Realize that many other people have their own challenges, which may be greater than your own, but all have the ability to develop a resilient strength to find a point of fulfillment and joy.

Chapter 10

MY OWN MANAGEMENT OF STRESS AND ANXIETY

I 'VE COMMITTED TO MULTIPLE JOBS, VOLUNTEER RESPONSIBILITIES, and deadlines to develop new courses. But this is not a new thing for me. As long as I can remember, I've taken on the maximal load that I could possibly bear. In high school, I committed to multiple clubs, church activities, and difficult classes, and still agreed to every new request, such as when the librarian asked if I would also design her main bulletin board in the hall. I remember that day thinking that I had already committed to so many things that I would have to stay up all night to get to everything. Yet I responded, "Of course!" That was the fifteenth thing I had agreed to add to my schedule that day, but I still made sure it was done and that it was the best bulletin board ever!

Every year I researched new big topics to submit to the science fair and social studies fair. This was not the little cardboard trifold project you might imagine. Beginning in July, prior to the next school year, I took over my parents' entire dining room with all the things I would need to pursue my vision for these projects. Picture three, six-foot plywood boards, stacks of research articles, art materials, and a few *Scientific American* journals that I checked out from the library. The projects were due in the late fall and early spring, but I was always excited to get started on new research every summer.

By my junior year of high school, I remember being at my friend Monica Franklin's house when her mom tried to help with the management of my extreme load of to-do lists. Her mom, Joy Franklin, was a successful businesswoman in real estate. She told me to write everything down I had committed to and then look at that list to decide what was really important to me—versus what was not—so I could remove them from the list. Of course, I thought they were all important, but I did try to listen to her point and allow more focus on my top priorities.

The result of always taking on more than what seemed to be physically possible was that I lived in some degree of stress at all times, determined to do it all. I stayed up all night at least one night a week, working on projects. Now I realize that was not healthy. By the tenth grade I was diagnosed with ulcers. But I still lived in a constant state of anxiety and refused to give up anything.

In college I changed majors a lot, so every quarter I would have to get permission from the dean to take classes above the maximal load, and I continued that plan through each summer until I finished graduate school. During my freshman year, my friends laughed when they saw that my day planner said *Nap 5:00–5:15 p.m.*, though it made sense to me as I had studied for most of the night, so grabbing a few minutes of sleep before my evening chemistry lab seemed to be the right thing to do.

Fast-forward to one of my first VP positions. One day, when I was twenty-seven years old and in charge of three states' nursing home therapy contracts, customers, and employees, I called to check on my mother in her small Louisiana town. She was stressed because that day she had just gone to the bank *and* to the post office *and* to the grocery store, so it had been a very long day of errands and she was exhausted. As I was listening to her, I thought, *Well, I had an early flight to one city to meet with employees, then I flew to another city and state to meet with other employees, then I flew to another state late that night to prepare for early morning meetings the next day.* I also utilized every moment of each flight to work on budgets and proactive action plans. But I was not stressed by my daily list of traveling and meetings across three states. Yet the three errands took all her energy, and she would have to stay home to recuperate the next day. So I guess it's all relative to what we are used to doing.

At another point, I was a thirty-four-year-old divorced, single mother of a four-year-old, was a vice president for a rehab company, had committed to four months of rehearsals several nights a week to be in an Easter musical at church, and then also decided to start training to run a marathon. My dear friend Kelly Hendren called and was always quite blunt in his communication with me. He said, "Is your head a brick? Why are you not seeing that this is not a good idea?" Eventually I agreed to give up on the marathon idea, but everything else was full speed ahead. I was determined to accomplish it all and would not listen to anyone who suggested I do otherwise.

Here's a typical journal entry from December 2022:

> *Today I have eight course deadlines due in the next six weeks for three different companies. I'm seeing clients for a clinic and have just agreed to a new home health patient, as well as to new client evaluations at the clinic. I spend one to two hours responding to emails every night for my volunteer organizations, followed by research for my courses until I fall asleep. My husband is facing great challenges with his radiation for throat cancer, and I'm going to physical therapy for a fractured right tibia and for tendonitis in my left arm. And there seems to be more to-do lists every day than hours in which to do them.*

In addition to exercise, my go-to strategy to get to the right mindset for such daily challenges is prayer. Rather than allowing myself to go into full panic about deadlines and fear, I also focus on scriptures such as,

> *Be anxious for nothing, but in everything by prayer and supplication, with thanksgiving, let your requests be made*

> *known to God; and the peace of God, which surpasses all understanding, will guard your hearts and minds through Christ Jesus. (Philippians 4:6-7)*

My dad and I used to discuss this scripture passage frequently, as it helped him through many challenges. That was also the case with his last big challenge of pancreatic cancer. By that time, we would even paraphrase it as "Pray about everything, worry about nothing." That's easier said than done in the biggest challenges, but it does bring the peace of God when everything around you is overwhelming and falling apart.

"Pray about everything, worry about nothing." That's easier said than done in the biggest challenges, but it does bring the peace of God when everything around you is overwhelming and falling apart."

I focus on this passage and pray to God with my requests to help me get everything done in time and with excellence; then I feel God bringing me peace. After researching what stress does to the heart, brain, and body over the last few years, I came to appreciate how Philippians 4:6-7, written by Paul thousands of years ago, promised that God would "guard your hearts and minds through Christ Jesus." It's really a miracle that God can decrease the anxiety—stop the flow of stress hormones, adrenaline, and cortisol—that would otherwise lead to mental debilitation and chronic inflammation and bring perfect peace and restore the heart and mind in times of stress. I mean, how cool is that?!

The next verse, which I often quote to myself and others, says,

> *Finally, brethren, whatever things are true, whatever things are noble, whatever things are just, whatever things are pure, whatever things are lovely, whatever things are of good report, if there is any virtue and if there is anything praiseworthy—meditate on these things. (Philippians 4:8)*

That is my direction each day. I quote this to friends and family members whose brains may tend to focus on what *might* go wrong in the worst-case scenario. There's a lot of bad and scary stuff in the world, but it's not healthy to dwell on that stuff. We can do what we can to make the world a better place, but we should remind ourselves throughout the day to think about what is good. And we can always find something that is good!

I have realized that anxiety is a part of my life. But if I keep it in check with prayer and focusing on how God is with me through this process, I can make it work for me and not against me. I thrive on accomplishing things and seeing finished products as work is achieved. I find joy in teaching groups of all sizes and hearing their responses about how they loved my class and now feel more equipped to do their jobs or to improve the quality of their lives. There are great rewards and victories from achieving all these commitments to which I've agreed.

Utilize strategies such as prayer, quoting encouraging scriptures, and exercising to manage anxiety. Realize a little anxiety can work for you and not against you. Channel that energy into getting things accomplished, and enjoy the satisfaction that comes from this.

Chapter 11

RESILIENCE IN THE BIBLE AND MOMENTS OF FAITH

T HE CONCEPT OF RESILIENCE IS REFERENCED IN THE BIBLE AS "endurance," "patience," and "long-suffering." It's a character quality that God grows in us through the process of sanctification. Hebrews points to the example of Jesus as our model of perseverance:

> *Therefore we also, since we are surrounded by so great a cloud of witnesses, let us lay aside every weight, and the sin which so easily ensnares us, and let us run with endurance the race that is set before us, looking unto Jesus, the author and finisher of our faith, who for the joy that was set before Him endured the cross, despising the shame, and has sat down at the right hand of the throne of God. (Hebrews 12:1-3)*

Faith builds resilience by helping us to see our current circumstances through a long-view perspective. It grounds our perspectives in hope and keeps us from being weighed down by trying circumstances.

Spiritual resilience is often referenced in research when scientists consider which factors are important in rising above adversity. It is the ability to sustain one's sense of self and purpose through a set of beliefs, principles, or values while encountering adversity, stress, and trauma, and by using internal and external spiritual resources. In seeking to better understand these constructs, Manning et al. (2019) asked the following questions:

Faith builds resilience by helping us to see our current circumstances through a long-view perspective. It grounds our perspectives in hope and keeps us from being weighed down by trying circumstances.

1. How do older adults experience adversity, and what internal and external resources do they draw on to deal with tragedy and hardship?

2. What is the relationship between spirituality and resilience for participants?

3. How did they experience their spirituality in relation to hardships, challenges, or adversities in their lives?

In this study, Manning et al. analyzed interviews with sixty-four adults who were willing to discuss their experiences with adversity. They then analyzed forty-six of the sixty-four interviews from participants who indicated that spirituality was an important resource for managing hardship. They found that people's use of spirituality as a tool to promote and maintain resilience in later life included five key domains: (1) reliance on relationships, (2) spiritual transformation, (3) spiritual coping, (4) power of belief, and (5) commitment to spiritual values and practices.[26]

Let's consider a few of the many examples from the Bible.

26. Lydia Manning, Morgan Ferris, Carla Narvaez Rosario, Molly Prues, and Lauren Bouchard, "Spiritual Resilience: Understanding the Protection and Promotion of Well-Being in the Later Life," *Journal of Religion, Spirituality & Aging* 31, no. 2 (2019): 168–186, https://doi.org/10.1080/15528030.2018.1532859.

JOB

The most commonly known biblical narrative on resilience is that of Job. Many of us know this story quite well. Job had a great life that included wealth and prosperity and was known by his livestock of seven thousand sheep, three thousand camels, five hundred yoke of oxen, and five hundred female donkeys. He also had a great family that included his wife and ten children. In a tragic turn of events, he suddenly faced many challenges and extreme trials, which included losing all his livestock (loss of wealth), severe illness, and the death of his three daughters and seven sons in a storm. His wife told him to curse God and die. His friends initially came to comfort him but eventually told him he deserved all the curses and suffering since they believed that God only sends calamities to wicked people. But Job said his greatest trial and challenge was his perceived loss of fellowship with God. Though the Bible doesn't reference how long these trials lasted, Job 7:3 references months of hardship. It could have lasted much longer, but all the losses happened quickly.

Job spoke words of expected renewal and a hope to die in peace, even when he did not feel peace. He frequently referenced his thankfulness for the peace of God, for his blessings, his family, and the blessings from God.

What were the points of resiliency for Job? Job sought God's renewal and peace:

> *"I thought, 'I will die in my own house,*
> *my days as numerous as the grains of sand.*
> *My roots will reach to the water,*
> *and the dew will lie all night on my branches.*
> *My glory will not fade;*
> *the bow will be ever new in my hand.'" (Job 29:18-20 NIV)*

Job spoke words of expected renewal and a hope to die in peace, even when he did not feel peace. He frequently referenced his thankfulness for the peace of God, for his blessings, his family, and the blessings from God. Verse 18 is clear that he expected to live a long life and enjoy a peaceful death.

Since Job lived in a desert, the analogy to water in verse 19 is significant: "My roots will reach to the water, and the dew will lie all night on my branches." In the desert there is no rain, so plants and trees gain moisture through their roots, which reach the underground water stored from the nightly dew. Job's words from verse 19 share his hope that he will continuously be nourished from his deep roots with God's presence.

In verse 20 Job states, "My glory will not fade; the bow will be ever new in my hand." His reference to "the bow" represents strength and resilience and is parallel to "strong arms" in Genesis 49:24 ("But his bow remained steady, his strong arms stayed limber," cf. 1 Samuel 2:4). Job expected to be energetic and youthful until the day of his death.[27]

We know from reading the rest of the story that God eventually renewed Job and brought him peace, which became his full process of resilience. We can read many other scriptures on how God brings strength through deep spiritual nourishment for renewal and peace:

The righteous person will flourish like the palm tree, he will grow like a cedar in Lebanon. (Psalm. 92:12)

But as for me, I am like a green olive tree in the house of God; I trust in the faithfulness of God forever and ever. (Psalm. 52:8)

He will be like a tree planted by streams of water, which yields its fruit in its season, and its leaf does not wither; and in whatever he does, he prospers. (Psalm 1:3)

One who trusts in his riches will fall, but the righteous will flourish like the green leaf. (Proverbs 11:28)

For he will be like a tree planted by the water that extends its roots by a stream and does not fear when the heat comes; but its leaves will be green, and it will not be anxious in a year of drought, nor cease to yield fruit. (Jeremiah 17:8)

Job encourages us to turn to God for deep-rooted strength for renewal, peace, and resilience during times when we may feel defeated, depleted, or exhausted from our current challenges and trials.

---

27. Robert Alden, *The New American Commentary, Vol. 11, Job* (Brentwood, TN: B&H Publishing Group, 1993), 284–85.

DAVID

David has been described in the Bible as the model king of Israel and, more importantly, "a man after God's own heart" (1 Samuel 13:14). The books of Samuel, Kings, and Chronicles describe his many successes. Though we read David's encouraging prayers and songs in the Psalms and may even think of him as a role model of greatness, he experienced great adversity and challenges as well, and he also made many mistakes.

We have all heard about David stepping forward with faith and a slingshot to kill the mighty giant Goliath when the army of Israel was afraid and could not fight him. He was only a young shepherd boy at that time, who had learned to protect his sheep from animals by killing those predators with his slingshot. But taking on a threatening giant with weapons and body armor required his extreme faith that God would work through him to do what seemed impossible to others. This action of faith became a well-known example for all of us who heard the story of how we too could overcome what seems to be the impossible challenges in our lives.

David was chosen by God and eventually anointed to be king and leader—and it would not be easy. He still had many more challenges to face. I wonder if his memory of God's miracle, using him to kill that giant with a small stone, maintained his faith to get him through all the subsequent challenges? He was a hero for saving Israel from the giant, and the reaction from the people makes it clear that they liked him more than King Saul. The Bible says that women began to sing, "Saul has killed his thousands and David his ten thousands" (1 Samuel 18:7). This shift of attention to David enraged Saul (1 Samuel 18:8), which made him want to kill David (1 Samuel 18:9-13). So David was forced to run for his life and to live in caves in the wildernesses of Judah for ten years. During this time David had an opportunity to kill King Saul, which would have resolved the problem of needing to run from him. But David chose not to do so, as it would only be right for God to give him the throne and not for him to take it: "It is God who executes judgment, putting down one and lifting up another" (Psalm 75:7). Therefore David still chose to show respect for the authority God had given to Saul.

Despite God choosing David to be king at some point in the future, this would not be an overnight moment of success. David would also have to go through an apprenticeship for seven-and-a-half years before he would finally become king of Hebron over the house of Judah (2 Samuel 2:1). Such biblical accounts remind me that God has a great plan for each of us, but it may not be in the timeline that we are wanting. We may want a big success today or tomorrow, but in God's timing, it may take a while. There may be lessons we need to first learn or challenges we must first overcome.

Fast forward to David's actions as the king of Israel. He utilized his power to do many great things, but he also made many mistakes. Examples include the time he took a census in violation of God's command (2 Samuel 24:10-17) or when he sexually exploited Bathsheba and tried to cover up his mistake by ordering the assassination of her husband, Uriah (2 Samuel 11:2-17). Another example is when David had chosen to support and protect a Calebite named Nabal, but when they got in a feud, David became angry and set out with four hundred men to kill Nabal and all his sons (1 Samuel 25). This shows David's arrogance and responsive temper leading to another potential giant mistake. Fortunately Nabal's wife, Abigail, saved the day with an act of kindness. She used great wisdom to dissolve David's anger and to save the day, for which he was later grateful, as he had gotten caught up in the moment. Abigail's action is another great story and an example to us all of how wisdom and kindness can save lives and prevent greater problems.

> **Such biblical accounts remind me that God has a great plan for each of us, but it may not be in the timeline that we are wanting. We may want a big success today or tomorrow, but in God's timing, it may take a while. There may be lessons we need to first learn or challenges we must first overcome.**

There are many other stories from the books of Samuel, Kings, and Chronicles, which share David's trials and victories. I am only citing a few examples. Some of his challenges appear to be the result of him doing the right thing and making good decisions, but others were from his human mistakes. He sought resilience through his faith in God and through God's mercy and forgiveness. As a result, he was king for forty years, including seven years over Hebron and thirty-three years over Israel.

David was a man anointed and chosen by God to do great things, but he was constantly challenged with long periods of adversity. He made mistakes but was shown mercy and forgiveness by God. He became known for finding strength and encouragement by praying and singing praises to God. Many of the Psalms share these praises, so we can read them and seek the same encouragement. Examples include the scriptures below. I find strength and hope in many of these, as I am able to say similar prayers:

> *In my distress I called to the LORD; I cried to my God for help. (Psalm 18:6 NIV)*

> *The LORD is my light and my salvation;*
> *Whom shall I fear?*
> *The LORD is the strength of my life;*
> *Of whom shall I be afraid?*
> *When the wicked came against me*
> *To eat up my flesh,*
> *My enemies and foes,*
> *They stumbled and fell. (Psalm 27:1-2)*

> *I will extol the LORD at all times; his praise will always be on my lips. My soul will boast in the LORD; let the afflicted hear and rejoice. Glorify the LORD with me; let us exalt his name together. I sought the LORD, and he answered me; he delivered me from all my fears. Those who look to him are radiant; their faces are never covered with shame. This poor man called, and the LORD heard him; he saved him out of all his troubles. (Psalm 34:1-6)*

> *I waited patiently for the LORD; he turned to me and heard my cry. He lifted me out of the slimy pit, out of the mud and mire; he set my feet on a rock and gave me a firm place to stand. He put a new song in my mouth, a hymn of praise to our God. Many will see and fear and put their trust in the LORD. (Psalm 40:1-3)*

> *As the deer pants for streams of water, so my soul pants for you, O God. My soul thirsts for God, for the living God. When can I go and meet with God? My tears have been my food day and night, while men say*

to me all day long, "Where is your God?" These things I remember as I pour out my soul: how I used to go with the multitude, leading the procession to the house of God, with shouts of joy and thanksgiving among the festive throng. Why are you downcast, O my soul? Why so disturbed within me? Put your hope in God, for I will yet praise him, my Savior and my God. (Psalm 42:1-6)

Be merciful to me, O God, for men hotly pursue me; all day long they press their attack. My slanderers pursue me all day long; many are attacking me in their pride. When I am afraid, I will trust in you. In God, whose word I praise, in God I trust; I will not be afraid. What can mortal man do to me? (Psalm 56:1-4)

My soul finds rest in God alone; my salvation comes from him. He alone is my rock and my salvation; he is my fortress, I will never be shaken. (Psalm 62:1-2)

JOSEPH

The story of Joseph includes his journey of resilience, trusting God, and forgiveness. Many of his adversities were despite his good decisions and his wisdom to do the right and ethical things, but they led to many long periods of trials and adversities. He was sold by his brothers into slavery because they were jealous of him. He was then in slavery in Egypt for a long period of time until one day when Potiphar's wife (Potiphar was the captain of the guards) accused him of unwanted sexual advances that he did not do, which resulted in his imprisonment. He spent at least twelve long years in prison before he would then be discovered by the Pharaoh and would become prime minister (Genesis 37-41).

Throughout most of his life up until that point, Joseph really focused on trusting and obeying God despite all the accusations against him. He experienced many years of loneliness, as things seemed to only progress from bad to worse with no hope of a future. Of course, he felt anger and frustration for these many years. Life seemed unfair from the time he was sold by his brothers at the age of seventeen up until he was chosen by the Pharaoh to have authority at the age of thirty. But he also experienced unexpected sources of help. For example, he never expected that the men he met in jail would be the ones who would help him to get the leadership opportunities over the nation. God always kept his hand on Joseph and had a really great plan for his life in the future.

There are many other examples throughout the Old Testament that show us how men and women persevered through extreme situations and rose to great blessings and renewal from God. Writing about them all would be another book full of their stories. But I also love scriptures and references from the New Testament. I speak these over my life while I'm driving or just getting through my day.

Philippians 4 includes several verses written by Paul, who seemed to live in a state of adversity. He wrote these words of encouragement:

> *I can do all things through Christ, who strengthens me. (Philippians 4:13)*

> *Be anxious for nothing, but in everything by prayer and supplication, with thanksgiving, let your requests be made known to God. (Philippians 4:6)*

> *Finally, brethren, whatsoever things are true, whatsoever things are honest, whatsoever things are just, whatsoever things are pure, whatsoever things are lovely, whatsoever things are of good report; if there be any virtue, and if there be any praise, think on these things. (Philippians 4:8)*

I have also found hope by reading the first chapter of James in the early hours of the day, as it often seems to give me new strength and encouragement for my day. It references the hope we have while experiencing trials and temptations that will come in our natural lives. Here are some of the scriptures that encourage me from James 1:

> *My brethren, count it all joy when you fall into various trials, knowing that the testing of your faith produces patience. But let patience have its perfect work, that you may be perfect and complete, lacking nothing. If any of you lacks wisdom, let him ask of God, who gives to all liberally and without reproach, and it will be given to him. But let him ask in faith, with no doubting, for he who doubts is like a wave of the sea driven and tossed by the wind. For let not that man suppose that he will receive anything from the Lord; he is a double-minded*

man, unstable in all his ways. Let the lowly brother glory in his exaltation, but the rich in his humiliation, because as a flower of the field he will pass away. For no sooner has the sun risen with a burning heat than it withers the grass; its flower falls, and its beautiful appearance perishes. So the rich man also will fade away in his pursuits. (James 1:2-11)

This next section encourages us to love and trust God as we experience trials and challenges:

Blessed is the man who endures temptation; for when he has been approved, he will receive the crown of life which the Lord has promised to those who love Him. Let no one say when he is tempted, "I am tempted by God"; for God cannot be tempted by evil, nor does He Himself tempt anyone. But each one is tempted when he is drawn away by his own desires and enticed. Then, when desire has conceived, it gives birth to sin; and sin, when it is full-grown, brings forth death. Do not be deceived, my beloved brethren. Every good gift and every perfect gift is from above, and comes down from the Father of lights, with whom there is no variation or shadow of turning. Of His own will He brought us forth by the word of truth, that we might be a kind of first fruits of His creatures. (James 1:12-18)

Finally, this Old Testament scripture seems to include the greatest reminders of God's plan for our resilience:

But they that wait upon the LORD shall renew their strength; they shall mount up with wings as eagles; they shall run, and not be weary; and they shall walk, and not faint. (Isaiah 40:31)

These many biblical references encourage us through the continuum of stress; whether we are slightly troubled or we may be terrified of the future, we can pray that God will bring total peace to our life and our family, and He can bring us a peace to stop the fears, stop the stress hormones, and tame the amygdala!

A FEW OF MY FAITH-BUILDING MOMENTS

I remember sitting in my living room at the age of five as my father lay on the couch in his weak state of illness. It was hard for my little developing brain to comprehend, but all I knew was that he had been a pastor of a church while simultaneously managing a full workload in the logging business. He loved God with all his heart and was a great community leader. But now he was dying due to cardiac complications from rheumatic fever. He was told to stop pastoring and give up his job since he had only a few weeks to live, as his complications had severely damaged his heart. That Sunday, I sat on the floor while my parents watched a church service on TV. My father especially loved hearing the Reverend B. H. Clendennen from a Beaumont Assembly of God church. When the service ended that day, they asked viewers to call in for prayer. My father called and spoke with Reverend Clendennen, who prayed a powerful prayer over him. The next few weeks are a blur to me, but they included my father's complete healing, a move to Beaumont, where his ministry continued with that church, a return to owning and running a business, and many blessings thereafter.

I've witnessed many miracles and blessings since that moment, which are too many to count. But those early memories of God's miracles that surpassed all circumstances and expectations

> I anticipate the moment that God is going to turn things around as only He can do. So I live and walk by faith while waiting for His perfect timing

have remained in my deep memories. Consequently every challenge I've experienced since that point is not seen as hopeless. Instead, I anticipate the moment that God is going to turn things around as only He can do. So I live and walk by faith while waiting for His perfect timing.

Fast-forward to a seemingly lost cause, no-win situation when I was in my early thirties. I was recently married to Ron, who was a new believer and who told me more than once that he did not grow up in a life of many faith-building miracles as I did. He sought to blindly trust God, even when he wondered how God could possibly step in and do the impossible. At that time I had a boat, which I had purchased five years prior. I was still paying a monthly note on this seventeen-foot Sea Ray ski boat that was being stored on a friend's land full of decay and ants, with a dead battery and on a trailer with flat tires—and I had five years of payments remaining. All of this was the result of a divorce and my ex-husband, who was "taking care of it" for me. This boat seemed to be worth nothing, but I had five years of notes remaining. So Ron and I cleaned it up, threw away the molded life preservers, aired up the tires, and moved it to our house. We put an advertisement out to sell it in the online classified section of the *Austin American Statesman*. And I prayed a sincere prayer and gave the situation to God.

Two weeks later, a man called from Chicago and said he wanted to buy the boat. Ron spoke with him and honestly told him that we did not even know if the motor worked since the battery was dead and we couldn't test it. That did not seem to deter this man. He still wanted to buy the boat. The following weekend, that man drove from Chicago to Austin, gave us ten thousand dollars in cash, and left with the boat and trailer. He later called us to tell us that in fact the motor did need to be replaced, but he took it on as a project.

Joy does not require the absence of disease, distress, or adversity.

This unbelievable event added to both my and Ron's faith. I had learned to live, believing in God's potential blessings, and now Ron began to see how such faith works. For many years thereafter, when Ron had difficulty with faith, I would cheerfully say, "Remember the man from Chicago who bought the boat that didn't run?"

In my experiences of walking by faith, and in my studies of how God brought resilience to people in the Bible, I focus on the knowledge that God is in control and in His own timing. I always realize a few other points, such as how things could always be worse and that change is a constant. So as we experience change, we should expect it, then learn to adapt to it and expect to thrive on it. From knowledge of these experiences, I know that joy does not require the absence of disease, distress, or adversity.

Recall from people in the Bible or from other people you know that victories over challenges may not happen quickly. Trusting the process and living by faith is required. Rejoice in the fact that God is in control, and He has great things in store for you, even though it may take a while to get there.

Chapter 12

A FAMILY MEMBER'S ILLNESS

I LLNESSES ARE A NATURAL PART OF LIFE, AS OUR BODIES WILL periodically become exposed to infections or breakdown for different reasons. Most people have experienced their own body shutting down due to the flu or an upper respiratory infection, maybe even serious infections that required hospitalizations. I've experienced a couple such serious infections, one that even led to sepsis, but eventually my body responded to IV antibiotics and recovered.

My husband, Ron, seemed to dodge the bullet of illness throughout his life until recently. He seemed to never get sick, and we sometimes called him the Energizer Bunny, since he was constantly productive either at work or around the house. He rarely even sat down, with the exception of football season, which finally gave him a reason to sit and watch a game.

Last summer everything changed. Ron went through his regular periodic cardiovascular testing, as he had developed high blood pressure a few years ago, but it was well managed with one medication. Then with an active lifestyle and a healthy diet, he improved his vital signs to the point that blood pressure medicine was not even needed. Since his father died at the age of fifty-six from a myocardial infraction (heart attack), it was a wise decision to manage any potential cardiac risks.

Following multiple cardiac diagnostic tests, Ron's cardiologist told him, "Mr. Milliken, your heart is perfect. I wish all my patients had such results!" But we went to a follow-up appointment a few months later after he experienced chest pains and swelling in his legs. I had just finished a two-year project where I researched cardiac rehab for a six-hour advanced course I was teaching for PT, OT, and nursing, so I was quite familiar with these symptoms.

The timing is never good to make these discoveries, and in this case, we were leaving for a long-planned trip to London the following week. But the cardiologist worked us in for an appointment and was quite concerned, saying Ron would need several additional tests to see what could have caused this sudden onset of symptoms. It was a Friday afternoon, so they decided to start with bloodwork, then run the additional tests the following week. It was also nine days before our flight to London, where of course I had a full eight days scheduled with itineraries for London, Paris, and Scotland.

The following day I was on my way to my hair appointment when I got a call from the cardiologist's nurse practitioner, who told me she had been trying to call Ron, but he was not answering his phone. Unlike other people during non-work hours, he is not one who always keeps his phone with him. On this day, he was shopping in a department store and had left his phone in the car. She explained that they found the cause of his leg swelling and heart pains: his hemoglobin was extremely low. She used the analogy of it being similar to a car with a brand-new engine (perfect heart) but very low oil (his blood), so it was overworking the engine and would eventually burn up if not addressed. She told me to take him to an emergency room as soon as possible for a blood transfusion.

This concept was not completely new to us, since Ron had been diagnosed with anemia a few months before, but everyone thought it was a bleed in his gastrointestinal tract. So a gastroenterologist had run every possible test to find a bleed, but again, everything looked "perfect," so there were no bleeds. They could not determine the cause of the anemia, so they sent him to a hematologist. But throughout those months of testing, his blood levels still maintained above the 8.0 level. On this day in May 2022, his hemoglobin was 6.5. That was the first of many transfusions to come. He would eventually require transfusions on a weekly basis.

Things escalated during this process when he was diagnosed with myelodysplasia syndrome (MDS), which means his bone marrow is not producing red blood cells. We were also told this is pre-leukemia and should be treated to prevent it from becoming acute leukemia. We were then sent to MD Anderson to participate in a clinical trial for MDS. Ron was accepted in the trial, which included taking a chemotherapy medication and having his blood checked twice a week for hemoglobin and platelet counts, with transfusions about once a week. The trial started in July. There were no typical side effects except decreased immunity. That was a bit of a concern, as we were technically still in a pandemic. But he continued working a lot, covering engineering projects throughout the Gulf Coast of Texas and Louisiana and succeeding in every way. At that point he rarely let me go with him to an appointment or a transfusion, as he maintained a high degree of independence and worked from his phone and laptop at the hospital.

I happened to go with him to a follow-up appointment with his leukemia doctor, who would tell him what they found on a recent test. Ron had told me about a lump in his neck, and I kept encouraging him to talk to his nurse practitioner on the next lab review. But he didn't think much about it until I asked him the third time to please ask someone about it. So when I went with him to this appointment in the MD Anderson leukemia department, I asked about the results of the diagnostic test of his throat and neck.

That's the day we felt the biggest shock. It was September 2022. We were told he has cancer on the base of his tongue and epiglottis with bilateral nodes on his lymph glands. Since I'm a speech pathologist and have treated many people with swallowing disorders, I knew too much about this. I vividly remember what I was wearing that day and how totally numb I felt about this information. When we left the office, I kept telling myself to just take one more step . . . and then another. Remember to breathe. I was in shock.

Several weeks passed without a treatment plan, as each member of the head and neck cancer team had to meet with Ron, and then they would all talk about how to proceed. One doctor told him only about a worst-case scenario of how he would lose all function from radiation and chemotherapy. Another doctor who was a surgeon told him he wasn't a candidate for radiation and chemotherapy because of his MDS, so she would just operate and remove the cancer. This really increased his hopes to get this over with and move on. But when I returned with him for the next visit, she said "never mind," he was not a candidate for surgery. She didn't tell him why, which made him very angry. He was in the process of telling her something, leading to his question he wanted to ask, when she put her hand up in his face and said, "STOP! I'm not finished with what I need to say!" I could not believe what I just witnessed. She told him he would have to have chemotherapy and radiation. This took him back to the other doctor's worst-case scenario discussion.

I kept telling myself to just take one more step . . . and then another. Remember to breathe.

An additional factor that escalated the whole treatment plan is that he is highly claustrophobic. If he is put in a confined space, he goes into full post-traumatic stress/panic attack mode. So he announced he could not do radiation because he researched the whole process and learned about the mask, which they make to fit your face and shoulders. Then they would bolt down that molded, tight mask over your face and to the table, where you can't move. The thought of it put him in full panic mode.

While I was teaching a scheduled webinar, Ron had a scheduled appointment with the physician/radiologist, Dr. Fuller, to discuss this radiation plan. He almost cancelled it because he was so angry with the last physician and was thinking about finding another hospital for a second opinion. But thank God he decided to go, just to tell the guy, "No way." I raced down to MD Anderson the second I finished teaching my online webinar and called him on the way to see how it went. I would still be able to join him for his next appointment with the doctor who was a chemotherapy specialist. I was thanking God as I drove and heard Ron tell me how much he liked the doctor and how that doctor was going to help him through the process. He described Dr. Fuller as "a tall Texan wearing authentic cowboy boots." He convinced Ron that he had gotten other people with worse claustrophobia through this, and he would get him through it as well.

Then we met the next doctor, Dr. Gillison, who was also very informative. Up until then, Ron was still angry at the surgeon who had suddenly changed plans without giving him a reason. Dr. Gillison was very helpful and explained a *lot*. She shared that he had probably had these cysts in his neck and throat for thirty or more years, but they stayed benign, as his immune system had prevented them from becoming active. Once he had started the clinical trial, it had reduced his immune system's defense, and the cysts had been allowed to become activated and became cancerous. She also explained something that I felt stupid for not understanding before, as I've studied the cardiac system and everything related to it for years. The reason he was not a candidate for surgery was that his platelets were too low. So if he had surgery, to include incisions in the epiglottic area (at the top of his trachea, going to the lungs), he would hemorrhage and aspirate to death on the blood. I should have thought of that.

Finally a plan was set in place to start radiation, only without the concurrent chemotherapy, to begin the week after Thanksgiving. We both felt a great deal of fear, mostly of the unknown of how this would go. They developed a great plan for him to get photon radiation therapy—not proton radiation therapy, as the rays would come from a big single arm above him rather than a confined tube. He could take a clonazepam pill twenty minutes before the therapy to reduce his anxiety, and the radiation would only last fifteen minutes. The radiation techs were amazing to count down the minutes for him so he could better predict when it was going to be over. It all went *much* better than he expected!

Throughout all of this, he worked every day and continued to function at a very high level, including traveling to different meetings and conducting Zoom calls for all parties of a giant deal he was facilitating. He was amazing! I would have wanted to go home and take a nap! But initially he scheduled all radiation for 6 a.m. so he could be back at work and not miss any meetings. He also continued to get weekly transfusions while working.

By his last week of radiation, it was the second week of January, and I told him I wanted to go with him since I knew he was getting very weak. I could see how painful his swallowing had become and that he had lost almost a hundred pounds. He was losing too much strength to walk and drive, but he continued to work, and his brain never missed a beat. He took very little pain meds because he didn't like what it did to his ability to think.

Then we experienced the next big snag. I was with Ron at a weekly appointment when he had to report his pain levels. He told the nurse that his throat pain was a level six, but it was a level ten when he swallowed. He also told the nurse that he was out of the medicine that helps to decrease the pain with swallows. Even though the medication had been called in to our local pharmacy near our house (an hour away from MD Anderson), the nurse convinced us that we must go straight to the ER for a "pain management system." He walked us to the ER and told them Ron needed pain management. We waited for hours in the waiting room.

I eventually went to talk to the head nurse and pleaded, "Please, let us go home because we can just pick up his prescription, and that will manage his pain."

The nurse said, "Oh no, he needs a transfusion because his hemoglobin is 6.9."

I responded, "No! 6.9 is normal for him, and that's not why we are here. We need to get home because he has to be back tomorrow morning for a radiation at 6 a.m. Then he'll get his regularly scheduled transfusion tomorrow afternoon." I also told him, "If we could just leave by 7 p.m., we could make it to get his medication from our local pharmacy before they close."

The nurse said we had to stay or we would be out of compliance. In retrospect, I *really* wish we would have left anyway, but we were afraid they would not continue treating him.

By the time we got to a little ER holding room, I asked to speak to another nurse and convinced him we did not need a transfusion but only something for pain so that he could swallow some nutrition immediately thereafter. They said they did not have any nutritional drinks, and it would take one-to-two hours to get something from the kitchen. Now by this time, we had been there all day, and he had only had one protein drink that morning since we thought we would be home by 2 p.m. and he could drink his supplement then. We had no idea we would be sent to the ER for the entire afternoon and evening.

Around 9:30 p.m. they received the supplement drink from the kitchen and proceeded to give him a meperidine injection with a hydrocodone/acetaminophen tablet. It was winter, so he was wearing long sleeves. They didn't think to ask about the 25 mg fentanyl patch he wore on each arm. I didn't know about them either at the time. Apparently until last week he had been given one 12 mg patch, but during the prior week's doctor appointment, the one he would not let me go to with him, he was to double the dose to 25 mg. I later learned that he had misunderstood what they prescribed; he thought they meant to put one on each arm.

Once he got the drink down around 10 p.m. they sent us home. The medication combination in Ron's body almost completely shut down his brain and body's function for twenty-four hours. After I drove him home, it took me a long time to get him up the stairs and finally to bed. The next morning, I woke up to learn that he had fallen during the night in the bathroom because he was so sedated. I really thought he broke a hip as he could hardly bear weight. He was disoriented, and he didn't know where we were. I drove him back to MD Anderson for his radiation appointment that morning, and while there, I took him to Dr. Fuller's nurse to discuss his new condition. Ron told her about the fall but that it had happened at the San Antonio airport while there to pick me up as I was flying in from Minneapolis. He was very confused.

After that experience, Ron refused the fentanyl patches and would not let anyone give him meperidine again. He regained cognition after a couple of days but still had a lot of pain from the fall.

I think oncology physicians may be more accustomed to treating end-stage cancer patients, so I've learned they give pain and anxiety medications freely. However, in all the courses I teach, I cite the research on how such medications are linked to very high risks. Maybe they are helpful to end-stage hospice patients but not to those who want to continue functioning. I am a strong advocate for Ron to only receive the lowest level of pain management that is actually needed, as overmedicating with opioids leads to multiple safety risks, decreased brain function, and decreased coordination, in addition to dry mouth, constipation, and decreased gastrointestinal mobility. Ron was also against any pain medications that were not absolutely needed, as he wanted his brain to function, and he's always been against medications unless they were absolutely needed.

The next chapter of difficulty began the week after radiation was over. That's when the most intense pain in Ron's throat peaked. He continued to lose a great deal of weight until he looked like a skeleton. This is a man who had always maintained high muscle function throughout his life and had always been very athletic.

Three weeks later we did our blood review. Everything looked great, and he seemed to be feeling better. So I felt OK to leave him and drive four hours to my dearest friend's mom's funeral in north Louisiana. I stayed in a hotel there before going to the graveside service the next morning. Halfway into my two-hour drive to the cemetery, I received a text from Ron, saying he was in the hospital. In the middle of the night, he thought he was dying with intense abdominal pain, so he called 911. Twice. But they did not answer. So he took three Tylenol and screamed in pain the entire way to MD Anderson at 2 a.m., where he was admitted for pneumonia, an intestinal infection, and a blood clot to his liver. I drove straight home for five hours without stopping and grabbed the things he would need for the hospital, such as clean clothes, his electric razor, and other requested items. Then my schedule for the next few days was to get up at 4:30 a.m., drive to MD Anderson, stay until 10 p.m., then sleepily drive home.

Even though I vowed to stay by his side, I still had many huge deadlines. I had committed to finishing multiple course deadlines for three different companies and for my state convention, as well as the post-tests and other required materials. I answered emails and texts all day long. I even conducted a webinar with a university program from the corner of Ron's hospital room, as it had been scheduled one month prior. There was *no* down time and no time for rest. This had become my life for several months now. Little sleep, massive deadlines, caregiver fatigue, and fears of the unknown future.

In addition to being his advocate with all the health care practitioners and worrying about his future recovery options, we were also both highly cognizant of our questionable financial future. In the past we both had high incomes from our salaries plus all my side jobs teaching at conferences. But my company deleted my position in May 2020, calling it a pandemic cut. So I then began work as an independent contractor working for multiple sources— but with no benefits. We greatly depended on Ron's larger salary and his insurance benefits.

That's where another overwhelming and crippling fear kicked in. *What if we lose all sense of security?* Ron had always told everyone he was healthy and sharp and wanted to work full time, at least until our son finished college. And then he wanted to keep working as long as he could after that. He wanted to help our daughter and her family buy their first house. We had many plans. But he was also known to give money away to many nonprofit organizations, churches, and missionaries, rather than save it. We had small 401(k) accounts but nothing ready to retire on. None of this was expected. *Fear* of the unknown and lack of long-term security was forever in our minds as we also tried to keep doing the best we could to get through each today. To get him through this illness and through our immediate problems.

Another factor is that we told very few people about his illness. For the first few months of the cancer diagnosis, he did not want anyone to know. I respected that. It was Ron's wish to not disclose any private information about his health status, and above all, he did not want anyone on Facebook or at church to know about it. I think it was because he was trying to process it all himself, and there were too many unknowns about how it was all going to be resolved.

> **Prayer opens doors of relief by giving all concerns and fears to God and acknowledging that He is Jehovah Jireh, our Provider, and He will not forsake me.**

So that was a lonely place to be. Finally he allowed me to tell only a few of our closest friends who could keep the secret and not tell others. But for the most part, the people with whom I interacted on a daily basis had no idea of what was happening in my life.

APPLYING RESILIENCE

What gets us through each day, each hour, each minute, when life is overwhelming? How do we recover from adversity? Sometimes that recovery process must be ongoing because just when you make it over one giant hurdle and can breathe a minute on the other side, the next big obstacle is looming above. Yet again, it is unbelievable. How will we make it beyond this next trial?

Prayer opens doors of relief by giving all concerns and fears to God and acknowledging that He is Jehovah Jireh, our Provider, and He will not forsake me. When I pray, I first thank God for all the big and small things that He has done for me up until this point, which builds and instills faith in what He will continue to do for me. Then I know that everything will be OK, and I need to stop fearing the unknown future. In my life I've had multiple miracles and amazing doors opened in areas that would have otherwise been dead ends. But through prayer and recognition of God's almighty power, I can tame my amygdala.

Faith. I relate to the premise by Manning et al. (2018) as I think how faith grounds my perspective in hope and keeps me from being weighed down by current trials and circumstances.[28]

---

28. Manning et al., "Spiritual Resilience," 168–186.

Scriptures also sustain me as they have been my foundation throughout my entire life. I have many go-to scriptures that I stand on, including those I mentioned in the previous chapter, but here is a verse that became a part of my life during this fearful experience with Ron's health:

> *Be joyful in hope, patient in affliction, faithful in prayer.*
> *(Romans 12:12 NIV)*

The other factors that I've learned to incorporate where possible are *exercise, sleep,* and *hydration.* I'll later share more about these and many other effective practices of resilience. But during this time, when I was at the "just put one foot in front of the other" stage, I did try to practice basic stretching, take walks around the hospital, keep my water bottle filled, and go home to sleep at night, as I knew the attempts to sleep in the hospital would leave me with no reserves to manage Ron's care the following day. Without these basics, I could have easily collapsed when trying to get through the long days, waiting on Ron and dealing with all the nurses, doctors, and therapists who might come into his room.

Laughter. I have always loved to laugh! It is so liberating and stress-busting to laugh! It releases stress, frustration, and tension. Now there were definitely days that did not include any hope of laughter, but honestly those days were the ones where I was having more difficulty letting go of the fear, which allowed my amygdala to get out of control with worry. If we allow such emotions to get out of control, we could easily spiral into a downward shift of self-defeat. And I absolutely do not think that's what God wants for us. He wants us to live in hope! To look beyond the present dark situation and to focus on the fact that He has overcome the world and that we should trust Him.

It is so liberating and stress-busting to laugh! It releases stress, frustration, and tension.

Since I chose not to tell all my friends about Ron's illness that was dramatically taking over our lives, I could go about my day, and they could still say hilarious things to make me laugh—God knew I needed that. I would later tell them I was afraid that they may look at me with sadness and even pity, and that's *not* what I needed.

Finding the good instead of focusing on the bad. Every day while driving back to the hospital, I prayed and tried to focus on what was still good and where we still had hope. Even when there was a *lot* of bad news, which could be so overwhelming, it was important to try to focus on any area of good. Again, these scriptures would come to mind:

> *Finally, brethren, whatsoever things are true, whatsoever things are honest, whatsoever things are just, whatsoever things are pure, whatsoever things are lovely, whatsoever things are of good report; if there be any virtue, and if there be any praise, think on these things. (Philippians 4:8)*

> *Do not be anxious about anything, but in everything by prayer and supplication with thanksgiving let your requests be made known to God. And the peace of God, which surpasses all understanding, will guard your hearts and your minds in Christ Jesus. (Philippians 4:6–7)*

> *Cast all your anxiety on him because he cares for you. (1 Peter 5:7)*

> *"Therefore, I tell you, do not be anxious about your life, what you will eat or what you will drink, nor about your body, what you will put on. Is not life more than food, and the body more than clothing? Look at the birds of the air: they neither sow nor reap nor gather into barns, and yet your heavenly Father feeds them. Are you not of more value than they? And which of you by being anxious can add a single hour to his span of life? And why are you anxious about clothing? Consider the lilies of the field, how they grow: they neither toil nor spin, yet I tell you, even Solomon in all his glory was not arrayed like one of these. But if God so clothes the grass of the field, which today is alive and tomorrow is thrown into the oven, will he not much more clothe*

you, O you of little faith? Therefore, do not be anxious, saying, 'What shall we eat?' or 'What shall we drink?' or 'What shall we wear?' For the Gentiles seek after all these things, and your heavenly Father knows that you need them all. But seek first the kingdom of God and his righteousness, and all these things will be added to you. Therefore, do not be anxious about tomorrow, for tomorrow will be anxious for itself. Sufficient for the day is its own trouble." (Matthew 6:25–34)

I'm always amazed how such affirming scriptures bring new life and hope to change my mindset. When the amygdala in my brain wants to take over my thoughts and cause fear and hopelessness, these powerful words replace those fears with peace and a profound sense of calm. So yes, as Paul says, it truly is a peace that passes all understanding. It's beyond my understanding how I could feel peace in a time of turmoil, but God is good, and He brings me a new strength each day.

In times of greatest trials, pray a simple prayer to ask God to carry the overwhelming load for you. Speak these positive, encouraging scriptures that tell us not to be anxious because God knows everything and has it all under control.

Chapter 13

THE NEXT STAGES OF ILLNESS AND CAREGIVING CHALLENGES

T HE NEXT MAJOR MEDICATION RISK OCCURRED WHEN WE HAD asked for a safe prescription to help Ron manage his anxiety. I was thinking that maybe a selective serotonin reuptake inhibitor (SSRI) like a sertraline or paroxetine might help him. All of these things happening to his body were quite traumatic, and he desperately wanted to gain his muscle back and return to work. So he was developing a great deal of anxiety. When he finally got an appointment with the only department at MDA that could prescribe such medication, it was in the supportive care services group (palliative care). MD Anderson does not ask you for a time that works in your schedule; they just book things for you, and you watch your portal to see what is scheduled. So there are frequently scheduled appointments at the worst or most impossible time, such as while you're in the middle of a transfusion.

This time, Ron's palliative care video session was scheduled while I was driving to Austin to speak at my state convention. I called him when I arrived to see how it went and was shocked to hear that he had been prescribed two medications that, when taken together, could cause serotonin toxicity: escitalopram and olanzapine. I suggested that he just choose one of them to start and closely monitor the symptoms to see if it helped or had significant adverse effects.

My amazing friend Jerry McDonald had offered to fly in from Florida to stay with Ron while I needed to travel to teach. Thank God he was there in my absence to help Ron through the next few days. Ron had chosen the olanzapine, which he started that Thursday afternoon. But over the next few days, he lost coordination, experienced decreased memory, and started to have new difficulties swallowing. Within two days of taking the drug, he looked at me and said, "What is happening to me?!" I learned weeks later that his dosage was too high.

I have studied and taught on the effects of different medications over the last ten years, so I know that antipsychotics have the most significant effect on coordination, such as what is needed for walking and swallowing. Many of these drugs also lead to significant cognitive deficits. So I was very concerned about this new order for olanzapine. But I thought the physician must have a plan, so Ron and I agreed to this plan on a temporary basis.

THE NEXT DIAGNOSES

Throughout my last thirty-five years in health care, which has included treating patients, researching the current scientific literature, and equipping therapists with evidence-based practice tools, I've learned that *one diagnosis often leads to another.* The human body is an amazing and a most perfect creation. But it is made of millions of cells, nerves, and connective systems. A problem at any one level may eventually break down in another part of the body, and managing one breakdown becomes complex as we're considering all the risks that may affect another otherwise perfect factor. So it feels like the fable about the boy sticking his finger in the dam to prevent a big break, which requires more and more "fingers in the dam," until at some point there are no more fingers. Not to say that many diseases are not treatable, but there's always a risk, so the complexity of the human body must be carefully managed.

When Ron was first diagnosed with MDS in June 2022, we were told that it must be aggressively managed to prevent it from becoming acute leukemia. He was eventually approved to enter a clinical trial at MD Anderson to get a chemotherapy drug with great promise. But that drug's only adverse effect was decreasing his immunity, which led to throat cancer. So he had to go off the clinical trial to be treated with radiation. It took two months for the team to decide and then get him on the schedule to start radiation, and then they told us we had to wait another two months after radiation for the MRI to prove he no longer had cancer before they could start him on another clinical trial. That meant they could not treat the MDS from October to March. Instead, they could only continue to check his blood levels every Tuesday and Friday, have him meet with a nurse practitioner to review his labs and any other new symptoms, and get weekly transfusions, since MDS caused his body to not make red blood cells. He anxiously waited for March 15 when he could finally get the MRI and go back to his leukemia doctor to start addressing the MDS again, all the time worried that he would otherwise get acute leukemia.

Then in late February, I had two big speaking commitments, including our big Texas Speech and Hearing Association (TSHA) convention in Austin that started with a board meeting and then progressed through an intensive schedule of courses, a capitol visit, teaching two courses, and attending important meetings and events, since I was president-elect for this large organization. Then I would drive home Saturday afternoon and fly to Seattle on Sunday morning to film four courses for MedBridge. All this had been planned many months before, so getting out of either event was not an option. Jerry McDonald, my dear friend of forty years, had called several weeks prior to offer to come stay with Ron while I was traveling, as he knew what my job required. That was such a God-sent blessing! Jerry totally understood caregiving, as he had recently retired from being a senior retirement center executive director and had also cared for his own mother until she passed away a short time ago. He's also been a very close friend to me since our first day of undergraduate school at Louisiana Tech and has remained a dear friend to our family. Jerry was able to fly in shortly after I left for Austin but had to fly home on Monday, prior to my return on Wednesday night. At that point, we thought Ron was recovering well from the radiation but just needed someone with him until his strength returned. But Bill Hines, another long-term friend of Ron's, had agreed to pick him up that Tuesday morning to take him for his regular Tuesday blood draws at MD Anderson. Therefore Ron had assistance each day that I had to be away.

I was filming courses for MedBridge all day Monday and Tuesday, with a flight scheduled out of Seattle on Wednesday. I kept my phone silent throughout filming, but when I checked it on our break for lunch, I saw Bill had called. I called him back to learn they were admitting Ron to the hospital. His white blood count was fifty-eight. I knew what that meant. His MDS had most likely progressed to acute leukemia. I compartmentalized my focus and returned to teaching for the afternoon without telling my producer or filming crew. I wasn't ready to share my fears and taint the filming process. The goal was to maintain high energy and to stay focused.

After the day of filming, I arrived back to my hotel to call Ron, who was still in the ER, waiting for a hospital room in the tower to become available. He had convinced Bill to leave him and go home, but no one realized he would be waiting for ten hours before he would be moved to a room. He was very frustrated.

I wasn't ready to share my fears. . . . the goal was to maintain high energy and to stay focused.

We stayed on the phone for hours, as he kept complaining that no one would bring him water, and I kept coaching him to hit the call light until finally, hours later, a nurse came in and brought him a cup of water. He was so angry.

I spent the next day flying home, as my flight left Seattle at 2:20 p.m. and arrived in Houston around 9 p.m. (with several delays). I took an Uber home and prepared a bag of things Ron needed, which I would take to the hospital early the next morning.

The next few days were even more trying. Waking up around 4:30 a.m. to get ready and drive in morning traffic to MD Anderson, then staying until late night, then driving home, barely able to think. The following is an excerpt from my journal of what was happening in a few days' time period at MD Anderson cancer hospital:

Friday: Yesterday they performed a bone marrow biopsy to give a more accurate assessment of acute leukemia, which would show the monocytes and blasts. Since Ron has already had two of these tests and they were extremely painful, he requested sedation this time. They gave him midazolam to sedate him, which knocked him out for the rest of the day, although we did wake him up for a few minutes to get him to eat a few bites of oatmeal. But he had great difficulty swallowing. The doctor had just told us this morning that Ron needed an aggressive medication to lower his white blood count and that it was critical that he receive a LOT of hydration to prevent damage to his kidneys. His fellow physician rounding with him also heard crackles in Ron's lungs. I knew he was probably aspirating on all water, so I feared what would happen to his kidneys. I requested an order for the speech language pathologist to come assess him. She concluded exactly what I suspected. He needed a nasogastric (NG) tube for all nutrition. But the technician who needed to come place it must have been extremely busy, as they were unable to come until after I left at 9 p.m. Early this morning I received a voicemail message from the charge nurse around 1 a.m., saying that he had refused the NG. Apparently he was finally coming off the sedation from the midazolam in the middle of the night when he thought they were trying to kill him by turning on the bright lights over his bed and trying to insert the tube down his nose.

Today Ron was more coherent, with better cognition and function, which was closer to normal. But it was a day full of procedures. First, I had to convince Ron that the NG tube was his only option for nutrition and hydration. But it was a rough procedure, so he had a death grip on my hand the entire time. Fortunately Courtney, the technician, was amazing and carefully talked him through the process. Other events of the day included an abdominal X-ray, a chest echocardiogram, physical therapy, a PICC line insertion, speech therapy, and a few visits by the physician team and the nurse practitioner. It took a while to get the chest X-ray, and then it took a while for the nurse to finally start nutrition through the NG, so Ron basically had no nutrition or hydration since yesterday morning before the midazolam.

Saturday: *Today Ron experienced adverse effects/ gastrointestinal reactions all day due to the new meds. But he also slept a lot, since he didn't sleep much the night before.*

Sunday: *Today included Ron being more confused in the morning. The physician team rounded and was concerned that he was now showing signs of kidney damage. They requested a CT of the brain, due to his new symptoms of slurred speech and decreased orientation, to rule out a stroke or a transient ischemic attack (TIA), but the results of this test determined his confusion was more so from the decreased kidney function.*

The bottom line from all these tests: he has acute leukemia and needs aggressive treatment with three meds: cladribine, cytarabine, and venetoclax. These medications presented greater risks of several adverse effects, some of which could lead him to the ICU for management. So he will need several weeks of hospitalization.

By the end of today, his kidney function had dropped significantly, so there was a stat order for the nephrologist all day. But we just waited. The decreased kidney function was causing significant confusion. He would mention names of his closest friends and then ask me how he knows them. I waited all day for the nephrologist to show up, but that never happened. The nurse said that because it was a Sunday, he sometimes doesn't make it in. The medication that helped to drop his WBC was causing his kidneys to fail, just as the doctor predicted.

Monday: *The nephrologist finally came to talk to us. Then Ron had a modified barium swallow study (MBSS) and kidney ultrasound. By the evening at 7 p.m., the nurse practitioner told me that Ron may need to go to the ICU, but they would keep checking blood gases. The hospital sent a guy named Sarik to be his sitter for the night due to Ron's extreme confusion.*

Tuesday: *The doctor said Ron would need forty-eight hours of continuous dialysis in the Intensive Care Unit (ICU). His hemoglobin was 5.8, and his platelets were 6. Roderick, his sister, prayed with us and encouraged us. By 2 p.m., we were finally moved to the ICU for a slow, continuous dialysis.*

Wednesday: *When I arrived today, Ron was barely talking. He was also very confused but was asking me to call our attorney. He said they were trying kill him here. I consoled him and told him they were all helping him. His eyes were huge, and he seemed to be very fearful. He knew who I was but otherwise was very disoriented. Metabolic dysfunctions are so hard on the body.*

Several people came in to talk to me this morning, including the nurse practitioner, the nurse, the nephrologist, and then the leukemia physician and his fellow. They told me he was doing well with dialysis, and they would take him off this afternoon to see how he responded at that point. Then he could do hemodialysis on an as-needed basis, rather than continuous dialysis, but he would need to stay in the ICU for another day or two.

Thursday: Today I arrived, and Ron was just lying there and not responding. He could only respond with slow head nods, but he could not speak at all. So they did an electroencephalogram (EEG) to measure the electrical activity in the brain.

MY ATTEMPTS TO MANAGE FEAR

My other journaled thoughts during this period of time:

Lord, tame my amygdala. Bring hope for the moment, even if tomorrow or some point in the future brings further loss. I need hope to survive this moment. To communicate with my children. And to have the strength and energy to be the caregiver and advocate that I need to be right now.

I made it through the intense pressure of multiple simultaneous work deadlines to research, develop, and teach courses, while being a caregiver over the last two months. But all the while I had more hope because I truly thought that I would support Ron through recovery from radiation for throat cancer. But these days are looking even darker. I must not assume the worst. I must focus on supporting him now and getting him the help he needs.

Lord, tame my amygdala. Bring hope for the moment, even if tomorrow or some point in the future brings further loss. I need hope to survive this moment.

Journal from Thursday 3/9/23:

Fears and more thoughts of worst-case scenarios are happening at this moment. I arrived at 9:30 this morning and tried to talk to Ron in my most cheerful voice, and he just stared at me. I asked the nurse at the station, and she said his vitals look good but he's no longer talking so they may need an MRI.

Three other practitioners came to speak to me about needing this MRI. I wanted it as well, to see what was going on, while fearing the worst. Has he had a stroke? What does that mean? I have treated or supervised treatments for a few hundred patients following stroke over the last thirty-five years. There are many possible outcomes from best to worst-case scenarios, but given his leukemia, MDS, and kidney function, I knew these factors would all affect his prognosis.

I think our human brain is geared to fear the worst-case scenario. And if Ron becomes unable to speak or be active, that would make him furious. He always said to not ever let him live like a vegetable. He wanted to remain active, intelligent, and working until he died. But his current status is not what any of us are able to understand. He was doing so well just a few days ago, until his kidney function started to worsen. The doctor said he would most likely improve his cognitive function after two days of dialysis. Vitals remained stable.

What am I going to do? What would I tell Jake and Alex [my children]? I am so thankful that Jim and Karen Burr will be here in a few days to get me through whatever the next steps are.

God, please help him recover from this situation!

I texted a few of my prayer warrior friends and ministers, including Pastor Mazz, Pastor George Lee Glass, Pastor Baker, as well as Pam Baker, Leah Mazzapica, Rebecca Alworth, Melanie Johnston, Tracy Winkley, Suzanne Bonifert, and Ronda Polansky, and asked them for prayer. Pastor Baker was also in Israel leading a group of fifty-three ministers, so he asked them to all pray as well.

ANOTHER PRAYER ANSWERED

By 5 p.m., the nurse came to report no indications of a stroke on the MRI! Praise the Lord, and to God be the glory! I could not stop praising God for this great blessing. Now we were back to treating the kidney function and acute leukemia, which suddenly sounded more doable.

After five days in the ICU, Ron was moved back to a regular room in the tower. He was thanking God all the way as the transport guy moved him via gurney to the seventeenth floor. He still had difficulty speaking, but it was more so due to his soft palate being covered with thick, dried blood, so his attempts to talk were very hyponasal, and his attempted speech was very distorted or not audible at all.

By the next day, he was talking nonstop, and he was well on his way to recovery, though he still had decreased strength and required assistance to stand. He was very weak and unable to walk or do normal activities for daily living. A range of different physicians continued to monitor Ron's kidney function, platelets, and hemoglobin levels, as well as give him IV hydration, NG feeding, and medications to manage and prevent infections. He also needed to work on building strength and function but only saw an occasional therapist every few days and only for a few minutes at a time.

CAREGIVING IS NOT ALWAYS APPRECIATED

For many years I've worked with caregivers of my patients in different health care settings and have taught several conferences to groups of caregivers. I've always thought of them as selfless and amazing people who will do anything to provide the best care and attention for their loved one. However, now that I am a caregiver, I'm understanding new levels of the toll it takes on them. While I've always stressed the need for caregivers to take breaks, care for themselves, ensure proper sleep and nutrition, and get some exercise, I hadn't fully realized the level of mental anguish that caregivers may experience.

Loved ones requiring acute care will frequently become angry, which is a natural response to their situation. They're losing control of their own bodies and are facing further losses due to their disease process. This is frightening, and their defense systems are triggered to kick in and fight for some level of control in their lives. This may

THE NEXT STAGES OF ILLNESS AND CAREGIVING CHALLENGES

cause them to become verbally or physically abusive to anyone trying to care for them. I've seen this response many times, and it is even worse if they are given antipsychotics to temporarily sedate them. In these cases, they will often lose coordination and swallowing abilities and then become more combative between dosages as they are waking up from the sedation.

Loved ones requiring acute care will frequently become angry, which is a natural response to their situation. . . . This is frightening, and their defense systems are triggered to kick in and fight for some level of control in their lives.

In Ron's case, he was used to being very intelligent and directing several million-dollar projects for his company at work, so feeling helpless in a hospital bed made him dream up big ideas of personal financial deals he should be making. As the caregiver, I was feeling the effects of him switching back and forth, from tearfully thanking me for being his advocate and for always being by his side through this extremely difficult time, to being very angry at me for asking questions about prior financial decisions, and from trying to dissuade him from making big personal banking transactions from his hospital bed.

Ron became very angry about the NG tube in his nose and wanted it taken out immediately, as it was driving him crazy. He was very thirsty all the time due to the dry mouth caused by his medications and recent radiation, which affected his salivary glands. Then further medications had adverse effects of dry mouth, which was very uncomfortable and made his speech even more difficult. He asked every doctor, nurse, and tech who entered his room to take his NG tube out. He told every hospital staff member who walked in the door that he needs the NG tube out and something to eat and drink before he starves to death. Each time I explained that they were not the correct medical personnel to ask, as swallowing skills are not in their area of expertise. I also explained that he is getting perfect nutrition from his NG tube and all the needed hydration from his

IV. I explained this about twenty times a day, but he chose not to hear what I was saying and then became angrier with me. Now he did have a modified barium swallowing study (MBSS) shortly after his NG tube placement, and the results showed he could have thickened liquids. But due to various levels of communication breakdown, and despite me asking different physicians to please reference that MBSS and allow him to have thickened liquids, he never received them. We never saw the speech pathologist again, despite many requests. Ron's anger about the whole situation was often transferred to me.

I'm now much more able to understand how the caring advocate receives the brunt of all the patient's anger, as they are the only person available for the patient to direct their emotions. It is a tough and emotional experience to go from the person by their side for every waking moment for long periods of time and sometimes feeling appreciated, to being the source of where all anger is directed, as if their loved ones' entire illness and degree of debility is all their fault.

When the battle is most intense, and your brain feels unable to function, seek the prayer of friends to sustain you. Journal to help you process your thoughts and to gain clarity. Meditate on God's strength pouring over you. You may be surprised at the resulting peace that passes all understanding as the result of prayer.

Chapter 14

ESTABLISHING
A NEW MINDSET

E ACH DAY SEEMED TO BRING ANOTHER CHALLENGE AND A NEW SET of fears, so I journaled my thoughts to obtain focus and faith. There were several points where I did not think I could handle one more thing, as it presented a sense of helplessness and a lack of hope. So many fears were colliding together at one time. I remember one day when I really felt the weight of it all more than ever. I could not get myself to focus anymore. I felt like I couldn't breathe. My daughter, Alex Laycie, had come down from her home in Tennessee, and she left the hospital room with me to go meet Melanie, who had driven all the way down from Kingwood to bring us lunch. After getting the bags of food from Melanie, we were walking back to the elevators, and I felt a new level of panic. I struggled to breathe. Alex became my lifeline. She walked me through some breathing exercises, spoke with a calming voice, then got me upstairs to the family lounge, where we sat so I could pull it together before going back to Ron's room. The following journal entry was written on March 19, 2023, which was the midway point of Ron's hospitalization.

After the increasing and overwhelming challenges from this past week, I am training my brain and taming my amygdala to focus on what is good, including the many blessings for which I am grateful and the anticipated blessings in my future. This takes me back to my ongoing motto of the last twenty-five years: God has me on a "need-to-know" basis. He has great unknown things in store for me, but He just can't reveal what they are yet, as it may be too great for me to handle or believe. Somehow everything is going to work out, and it's going to be really amazing. I am picturing myself looking back on this moment many years from now, when things are much better and more secure. Some people may think that I have a "Pollyanna" attitude and that I'm not living in reality. But I am highly aware of all the reality in our lives, which includes debt, extreme illness, potential death or long-term illness and caregiving, and further unknown factors. Therefore I am definitely not pretending that such realities are not happening; I'm just choosing to focus on what's good rather than what is bad.

Another factor in seeking a new mindset is how I was so very grateful for the quiet encouragement from friends, which is priceless! Granted, I could not tell most of my friends about Ron's illness based on his wishes. So only the few people who knew were those who sent me words of encouragement. Another advantage of only telling a few people is that I did not have nonstop texts asking me how we're doing. My life was already overwhelmed with to-do lists, so the need to respond to so many texts and emails throughout the day would trigger an anxiety attack because there was just not enough time in the day. But the great thing about friends is when they send a word to encourage me, or even something to make me laugh, they do not expect a response, which means I could glance down at my phone, smile, and not have to step away to respond.

For example, my friend Karen Burr always knows what to send at the right time. That seems to be one of her special powers. One day I was walking through my typical hospital day of being in Ron's room, trying to help him, and trying to keep ongoing communication with the many doctors, nurses, and different health care people coming in and out of the room. I was exhausted, overwhelmed, and trying to stay positive. Then Karen sent me a cartoon graphic of a frazzled woman that said,

Yesterday: Fixed my hair and make-up. Saw no one.

Today: Looked like Jack Nicholson from the Shining. Saw all the people I know. All. Of. Them.

I cannot help but laugh when she sends these to me. Laughter overrides all stress hormones and anxiety, so it is very good for the soul. She would also send scriptures and devotionals, which were encouraging as well. As I was in the midst of what felt like a personal crisis, this simple text made me laugh, which broke the cycle of the flowing stress hormones of cortisol and adrenaline.

I am blessed to have many great friends who have been very kind and helpful. Jerry McDonald volunteered to come and stay with Ron at home in late February so I could travel and teach. I'm so grateful to Michael Grant as well, who offered his constant support from Fort Lauderdale. Then Jim and Karen Burr came and stayed with me after Ron had been in the hospital for a week so they could help me with things at home as well as go stay with Ron at the hospital one day so I could work. Bill Hines helped with transporting Ron, visiting him, and offering great support along the way. Jake (my son) was very helpful to come home for the week of spring break and go with me to the hospital most days and help me develop a spreadsheet of bills to pay on their respective dates.

My friend and colleague Suzanne Bonifert has contributed many unexpected blessings. We have been colleagues through our Texas Speech-Hearing Association (TSHA) committees and the executive board. I had tried not to tell any colleagues or church friends about Ron's illness, as I didn't want to use this challenge as an excuse for my own missed deadlines. I also wanted to keep everything "business as usual" as much as possible to keep work tasks flowing as they should. But I finally felt the need to tell Suzanne, as I needed to let her know why I would be out for a few hours and unavailable for a joint project. So on January 12, I emailed her a synopsis of what had been going on in my life, including a summary of the fears and related challenges we've been experiencing on a daily basis over the past several months. She immediately texted back with the most amazing support and subsequently began to text prayers, scriptures, and devotions to me almost every day. Sometimes they would be written texts or photos of scriptures; other times they would be a recording of her reading a scripture or devotion. It's been quite miraculous how, when I would finally get a minute to read the text or find a quiet place to listen to her audible recording, it would be the most perfect word of encouragement that I needed at that very moment.

I have many other amazing friends who have been there for me, including Tracy Winkley, my college roommate and always the voice of reason. I've called her many times on my late-night, hour-long drive home from MD Anderson, exhausted from the day and needing to talk through all the new problems of the day. Then my friends Ronda Polansky and Donna Fitzgerald-DeJean, who are speech pathology long-time friends, became constant sources of support. Melanie Johnston, another speech pathology friend who owns the clinic where I was working, became a constant daily encouragement and facilitator for so many things that I was confronting. My fellow Texas A&M Kingwood Humble Aggie Mom board members (the local chapter of moms of past and present Texas A&M students) were also like a sisterhood to me, and I know they were praying for me and sending their kind thoughts and prayers. That was my third year on the board, and they were all rallying behind me in support.

And though the prognosis was not good . . . I decided to be thankful for every day that I had with him.

I'm also so grateful to my pastor friends, who have been personal friends to Ron and me. These include Pastor Frank Mazzapica and Pastor Jon Alworth, who both came to the hospital a few times to sit by Ron and offer friendship and prayer. Their wives, Leah and Rebecca, respectively, have been my dear friends throughout this process—coming to visit and even spending the night on the couch by Ron's bed when he was unconscious in the Palliative Care Unit while I went home to rest, in case he woke up that night and tried to talk. I'm thankful to Pastor George Lee Glass, my running partner of forty years prior, who let me call him at 5 a.m. while I was driving back to MD Anderson on different mornings. I needed to process what was happening, and he's the only one who was awake at that time of the day and could pray over Ron and me.

So many people have been there for me without expecting me to call or text with frequent updates. There are so many other friends who were only a phone call away, but Ron wouldn't let me tell them what was happening. And though the prognosis was not good for Ron, I decided to be thankful for every day that I had with him. The following month would be our twenty-third anniversary, and there had been many great times throughout those years.

I am very thankful to Ron's company for continuing to pay his salary through this hospitalization and for continuing all his benefits, including our family health insurance. This was a huge blessing! I realized it may end at any point, but I thanked God every day for that blessing.

Focus on the blessings in life, including supportive friends and resources, rather than on the many overwhelming fears and worst-case scenarios that are happening around you. Purposefully shifting this focus allows your brain to function again and stops the constant release of debilitating, negative stress hormones.

Chapter 15

RESILIENCE THROUGH
THE NEXT STORM

S TEPPING AWAY FROM THE PERSON YOU LOVE AND FOR WHOM YOU
are caring allows greater reflection on reality and prevents
escalating problems to higher levels. I was extremely fortunate to have
other resources there for Ron while I took my first day away from the
hospital. He had great nurses and a hospital staff that would stay on
top of all levels of his care. My friends Jim and Karen Burr were in
town many times to help for a few days, so they provided the needed
visiting and outside support so I could go to the clinic and work for
the day, go buy a new dryer when ours just stopped working, and run
a few needed errands. Getting away from the hospital and out in the
sunshine was so refreshing!

What follows is a summary of my journaled notes from 3/12–
3/18:

> *The next week brought more surprises at home. It's a long and
> sequential story, but my dryer stopped heating, so I had to
> go to Lowe's to buy a new dryer for $600. When the delivery*

guy arrived, he smelled a gas leak. That led to me calling the gas company, having them turn off the gas, and getting the plumbers to come out, which led to a $6,000 bill to replace all the leaking gas pipes throughout the house. By that Saturday it was all fixed, but the gas company was closed until Monday so I continued to be without heat during the evenings when I was home from the hospital. And though it

Stepping away from the person you love and for whom you are caring allows greater reflection on reality and prevents escalating problems to higher levels.

was mid-March, we experienced an uncharacteristic, brief cold front, so the outside temps dropped down to the forties and then the thirties before Monday. My house temperature was fifty-two degrees. I was also attempting to manage other household lists that Ron would have normally handled, such as gathering all the many complicated documents to take to the accountant for our taxes and addressing issues with the pool and other general home-related things.

I drove down to MD Anderson that Saturday morning, but Ron spent the morning being angry at me, since I was trying to discuss our financial situation. But in his efforts to seek some sort of control in his life, he was texting and calling people to buy things and order new and unneeded landscaping services and other costly things. My attempts to discuss plans for us to decrease spending resulted in Ron's escalated anger, and he told me to leave.

By Saturday afternoon I was feeling the stress of caregiving, escalating debt, being screamed at, and going home to a lonely house without heat and without a warm shower.

The next few weeks were not chronicled each day in my journal. I no longer had the time or mental focus to type the summary of each day. Ron's health continued to decline, and each day seemed to bring a new set of complications. He developed a blood infection, for which he needed intravenous antibiotics with further severe side effects. He was transferred back to ICU several times, then back to a different hospital floor and room. On one of the transfers back late one night, the nurse completed a head-to-toe skin assessment and found a wound on his buttock. His skin integrity was poor, he looked like a skeleton, and he was rarely helped to a seating or standing position anymore. He was now on dialysis three times a week, which he hated. That included transport taking him to the dialysis floor and leaving him in a tiny room to lay there while being connected to all the tubes. I sat beside him each time. Since he was also still getting blood transfusions every few days as well as a catheter and an IV drip, he sometimes had all these tubes connected simultaneously in the dialysis unit. He hated being in that state of debility and lack of control. He had always perceived himself as being a strong athlete with perfect health—invincible to such a demise.

Finally the day came when his leukemia doctor decided they would do another bone marrow test. If the results showed the leukemia to be in remission, then he could go to an inpatient rehab center the following Monday to start building back his strength. What great news! The doctors even convinced me that I should go to my scheduled National Academy of Practice (NAP) conference in Washington, DC, for that Thursday through Sunday. I had otherwise decided to cancel this trip that was scheduled six months prior, but they convinced me that it would be good for me to get away, and my friends Jon and Rebecca promised to visit Ron every day. While I was away, I got the promised two-to-three calls each day from the physicians regarding Ron's status. All was well until that Saturday afternoon when I received a call.

I left the meeting room to go into the hall. I was told the leukemia was back, and Ron had agreed to more treatments of the IV medication. I tried to get an immediate flight back to Houston, but there were storms and high winds in the area and all flights were cancelled. I was up early the next morning on the phone with United Airlines. Then, after two hours on hold and then speaking to an airline agent, I finally got a noon flight out. I texted Ron to tell him I would be there soon, and he responded with, *I've stopped all treatments.* What?! He was done. He couldn't take all the treatments anymore and decided this was no way to live while the prognosis was still very poor. He would later tell me that adding the medication back made him feel as though yet another bus was running over him.

On the flight home I felt a state of nonstop panic. I had called both my children to let them know what was happening. I talked to Alex in my hotel room, and I left a message for Jake to call me. I remember not being able to talk without crying, so I held it together in the airport until Jake was able to call me back. By that time I was at my gate, and a flood of tears came rushing in. By some miracle I was upgraded to first class, so I had a bit more privacy there. I watched a movie to distract my attention from reality and to yet again compartmentalize until I could be alone and let the tears continually flow.

After arriving in Houston, I drove straight to the hospital, and my friends Leah and Rebecca were there with Ron at his bedside. He had perfect cognition again. He was not connected to any tubes. His NG tube was out, and he was speaking with great objectivity. He spoke to me with compassion while I cried. He said, "Now I know this will be hard for you, just like it was so hard when your father died. But you'll be OK." We all talked for several more hours, and he was back to his normal, quick sense of humor. I left late that night and returned the next morning, hoping to have some one-on-one time with him to talk about our lives together these past twenty-three years. But when I arrived, he was in a coma.

I sat beside him and cried for hours. By 2 o'clock that afternoon he was moved to the palliative care floor. They called it their "Supportive Services" floor. Shortly thereafter Jerry arrived from Florida; then Tracy arrived from LA. We sat by Ron's bed, watching him in his unconscious state. Finally around 8 p.m. we were going to leave when Ron woke up and asked Tracy to move his legs, as he knew she was a physical therapist. She did some passive range of motion with his arms and legs and then helped him to sit up. He then proceeded to speak for hours, starting with asking Tracy how her boys were doing and then asking Jerry how his family was doing. He thanked them for always being there for our family and for being good friends to himself and to me.

The following day we all returned, but again he was in a coma. Leah and Rebecca came that evening. Ron did not stir. They decided to spend the night on the nearby chair and couch in case he woke up again so we could leave and go home for the night. The following few days, he did wake up. By this time Jake and Alex were there. We had two full days of family time, where we all sat together in his room and laughed and talked about our favorite family vacations. The doctors kept pulling me aside every day to basically tell me I needed to find a new placement for him, since this floor was only for the short term. They were giving him no treatments, so he couldn't stay here. Jerry helped me to interview different hospice companies, but they were all saying he would have to go home. Ron would tell me, "Don't let them trick you into putting a hospital bed in our house. That would be too much for you." I didn't know what to do, but I knew that patients often "rally" before they die. I've seen that through all of my career with our nursing home patients. They get better for a few hours or a few days to communicate and feel good one last time; then their bodies shut down and they pass away. I asked the hospital staff to please let him stay through the weekend, and they agreed.

Alex had to tell Ron goodbye and that she loved him on Friday night, as she would need to drive home early Saturday morning. Then on Saturday morning, when Jake, Jerry, and I arrived back to Ron's room, we learned that he had a rough night that included agitation, so they gave him a low dose of haloperidol. He was no longer responding and seemed to be struggling to take his last breaths. Jake arrived at the room first since we dropped him off before we parked the car. Two hours later, as Jake and I sat by Ron's side, holding each of his hands, he breathed his last breath.

I sought resilience over the next few hours and days by clinging to the directions of Jerry and Tracy to get through one step at a time. Rebecca and Leah came over. Tracy created two slideshows for the funeral and also created the funeral program to take to the printer. Jerry worked nonstop to help me organize bills and accounts and to make the initial needed calls, including Ron's boss and other friends of his who I knew would want to know what happened. Jerry and Tracy both went with me to the funeral home to plan details, and we had it all planned out by the time Pastor Brenda and Pastor Michelle arrived to discuss details for the church service. I typed the long Facebook post, as the whole world was now allowed to learn what had been going on. I then typed the eulogy that I would read at Ron's service. Each new task brought a new level of harsh reality.

> **I focused on physical, spiritual, and then emotional resilience to be able to move forward.**

Jerry went with me on long walks in the beautiful weather, which was so good for my soul. He and Tracy made sure that I ate something. This was the beginning of the next chapter of resilience. I focused on physical, spiritual, and then emotional resilience to be able to move forward.

When realities and worsening circumstances escalate, focus on getting through one minute at a time. Allow friends to help you through these moments. Add movement, such as long walks if possible, which helps the brain to process and to function better.

Chapter 16

WHEN TRAUMA AND GRIEF COINCIDE: RONDA'S STORY

S OME WHO KNOW RONDA MAY THINK SHE HAS THE PERFECT LIFE. She's beautiful, has the perfect husband and son, is a business owner, and has mentored many young professionals over the last thirty years. But multiple adversities affected her all at the same time. She shared the following account of how she struggled beneath the weight of it all.

> *Since 2020, not only did the world go into panic mode due to a pandemic but my son suffered a life-threatening brain injury requiring brain surgery and rehab, and my mom was suffering many years of the devasting effects of full-blown Alzheimer's that was unforgiving up to the very end. Mom lay in bed, contained in a shell of fifty-five lbs. of flesh and bone, with inhumane vitals of 40/80 and four breaths per minute for several days. She was a living, breathing corpse, with rigor*

mortis setting in. Something you can never unsee. My dad chose to give up on life, and I watched him wither away with no will to live for me or his grandson. It wasn't just one thing that caused this effect on me but rather a series of loss over and over again, and instead of recuperating and being able to take time needed, the trauma injuries were never given time to heal, and they began to compound.

In 2020 when Caden was severely injured, I went to a place I can only describe as an empty, endless, vast space. As a mother, your child is your heart walking outside your body, and he was broken so I was as well, but I could not let any of that be seen. It was COVID, and as he lay in the hospital, I was not allowed to be at my son's side. There is some indescribable, divine connection to a human being that was once literally an extension of your physical body, an appendage that grew and separated from you at nine months. On that day, 02/02/02, life stopped being about me and became all about him.

Being a mom means more than having given birth to a child. It's loving and knowing a soul before you even see it. It is carrying and caring for a life completely dependent on you for survival. It is giving air to the lungs that grew within you and sight to the eyes that will never see what you see in them.

That little, small mustard seed of faith was all I had. Steve came home from the ER and slept as we waited in the wee hours to hear about Caden's declining or improving condition. I was awake, unable to close my eyes for a total of forty-eight hours in this place of emotional numbness. "Why" is a question I feel always requires an answer. But my life had become a place of so many "whys," and this was one that had no response. It was a silent word that tormented me in many ways, but I chose to ignore it most of the time.

After Caden's brain surgery to fix a severed artery/bleed and a fractured skull, the months of July, August, and September in 2020 came and went in a blur of recovery and rehab. Caden healed miraculously. My parents' unending saga never stopped, and it just continued to decline.

I took on a lot of emotional endurance I did not know I even had. I had become exhausted trying to be stronger than I felt. I found out you can be brave, strong, and broken all at the same time. Yet in the end, when I needed the most support, even on a professional level, I was only permitted sporadic days to take care of what required my attention, including myself. It is funny how day by day nothing seems to change much, but when you look back, everything was different.

I took on a lot of emotional endurance I did not know I even had. I had become exhausted trying to be stronger than I felt. I found out you can be brave, strong, and broken all at the same time.

My health declined with diagnoses exacerbated by stress levels, my emotional state altered, and my reflection on life and time had been redefined. Watching myself become a shadow of someone . . . it is difficult to hide, especially when you are running from what you feel inside.

Trauma occurs when we encounter situations that are unusual, are unexpected, and go beyond our capacity to deal with them. The effect will depend on each person and on personal variables, such as our history, our social environment, or the moment we are in within our life. I have a hard time explaining my existence during the past two-to-three years and even now. There was trauma and then there was grief, and both existed during and after all of these. It's complicated but very real. It is a silent presence. It forms who I was through the pain and outlines who I am today. My past is now my armor, and I have a hard time taking it off even though I am told the battle is over.

The wave of this emotion comes in like an ocean tide—some are strong enough to lift you off your feet uncontrollably as you struggle to stay afloat, and others nudge you along as you give into the natural force. No matter the feeling, oddly it becomes an imposter of support. Most have strong feelings of shock, anger, fear, guilt, or grief. I felt them all. I guess some people start to feel better as they make sense of what is happening or what happened to them. I felt overwhelmed and trapped by intense emotions that did not subside.

Trauma is typically thought of as something physical, such as a brain injury, but it can be the emotion brought from feeling or seeing something traumatic. You can be present for it in many forms. Watching trauma envelope your child, requiring life-saving measures within minutes and hours, was ironically similar to watching Alzheimer's physically rip through the flesh and mind of my mother's body over the course of years, and was oddly similar to watching the life being sucked out of the beating heart of my father. The trauma I watched them endure transferred to my own personal, internalized trauma.

Prolonged trauma severely impacted my quality of life. Of course it is all in how we respond to it, they say. Relentless stress, in simple words, was characterized by the constant feeling of stress. This I could not run from as much as I tried to ignore it and exist with it. Trauma seemed to increase my pain threshold. This was, if I think about it, a very intelligent way my body reacted to protect me from further emotional and physical damage. My body was prepared for fight or flight against perceived danger/ trauma that was either before me or was to come. And when neither of these two were an option, my body went into freeze mode. My "freeze" reaction was similar to a mouse "playing dead" when caught by a cat, as they realize they can neither fight it nor run away from it. I sat quietly with it, mostly at bedsides, hour after hour, day after day, year after year, silently.

During this trauma, grief eventually pulled up a chair to the gathering. Grief was the result of how trauma was changing my life in these years and the connection I had to those I cared for. There is an unspoken cultural script to play when you grieve. You must exhibit enough sadness that if someone sees you, they don't think, She doesn't care very much, *but you also cannot be sad too long, as people's sympathy for you will expire at a certain point, whether you are fine or not. People love seeing others overcome levels of adversity, and I have successfully played that part for a long time. My reflexive response is always, "I'm OK," "I'm good." I may have always looked like I carried it well, but it did not mean it was or is not heavy. Some personal experiences are beyond words, but the one thing I know for sure is that any attempts to explain it or even attempts to comfort someone will always be imperfect to the reality. There is a common place between yelling for help and a place of hallelujah. I trained my mind to be stronger than my emotions, or I would lose myself to them every time.*

The trauma caused me to miss out on things in life, which led to feelings of great loss—loss of people, loss of time, loss of so much that was unretrievable, loss of me. The body will say what the mind doesn't. In other words, it was my bodily expression, through certain symptoms, of certain emotions and feelings that I was not quite able (or ready) to cope with in an emotional way. The response we have to our trauma severely impacts quality of life. The relentless stress, in simple words, was characterized by the constant feeling of stress. These high levels of stress became a regular part of my routine, but the truth was that it was having severe consequences on my health and emotional state, making me more vulnerable to developing physical health problems, including inflammatory effects and autoimmune illnesses. My body began attacking itself inside. Camouflaged from everyone. When I had anxiety and difficulty sleeping and concentrating, and I felt depressed, feeling irritable was the easiest, more common reaction. And yet people still questioned why I had these responses, as they expected me to have "gotten over this; enough time has passed." Yet it was just another one of my body's inner responses to years of experience with everyone's trauma.

Let me be clear that the effects of trauma can last for a long time, and it can also come and go. "Time heals all wounds" is the quote that comes to mind as so many people gave that to me as a prescription to all of my thoughts and feelings. No amount of rushing this process is going to make me heal faster or better; in fact, it will do quite the opposite. Grief does not shrink within us; we grow around it. Right now, I am in a happy middle. There is/was no happy ending with either of my parents. I feel joy, and I still feel sorrow, all at the same time. Some days I wake up and am grateful there is no more suffering. I am thankful for Caden's recovery. But then I am angry at the whole process we had to endure for so long with the outcome of my parents' deaths being so horrible and final and yet so triumphant.

No amount of rushing this process is going to make me heal faster or better; in fact, it will do quite the opposite. Grief does not shrink within us; we grow around it.

You cannot walk through life with toxic positivity. That type of forced emotion attempts to erase real life because grief is what everyone risks for love. Moving forward from it does not mean there won't be more of it. It only indicates that we are internally wired to overcome adversity in a fallen world. You set yourself to be the best version of yourself you think you can be. Letting go of experiences can be frightening, as it defines and shapes a period of life. What was or has been will not be forgotten or overlooked but will be put safely on the proverbial shelf, available to revisit or use as a resource any time you want to or need to. When a traumatic experience occurs, I believe it affects a person on a cellular level, as the body's cells have memory receptors. This experience makes an imprint (memory) on a person's soul, like an X-ray or a negative of a photo for those who remember what those are. You cannot unsee. I realized that trauma wears many hats, has many faces, and uses many names.

I feel like, because I am saved and functional, that it's OK to keep up appearances though I am very much broken and sad. It's not an insufficiency on the part of Christ but rather a lack of awareness or at least of courage on my part to go back in and allow the pain of uncovering those old hurts in order that I might heal. It's a bit like a surgery to re-break an old fracture so that it can begin to heal correctly. We avoid those situations because we know there is going to be pain involved. I got enough of it the first time around. I know the full measure of my pain and can compensate and cushion the known. It's scary to venture past that threshold of knowing, so I stay broken—either out of fear, out of guilt, or out of dread, or I think I am just too tired to pull up out of the ditch of despair. I cannot do this in a day or a weekend and quickly wipe those tears to go back to the reality of my life within the next few hours or the next couple days. I have sacrificed me.

Trauma *by any other name is still* trauma, *and* grief *is still* grief. *I pray that I will have the ability to discern who my battle is with. I must recognize who and what it is I am fighting against. If you don't know who your adversary is, how can you effectively do battle against it? Faith is all you have when there is nothing left to hold on to. I will go forward in faith with the full expectation that I will receive everything that He has for me as His light outshines the darkness, and hope for a brighter day anchors my soul.*

And somedays . . . it will take work to just be OK.[29]

Trust the process of faith, and accept God's comfort when you're experiencing the greatest levels of trauma and grief. The healing process will take time, but a focus on God's peace that passes all understanding will get you through that process. Know there is a brighter day ahead.

29. Full story used with permission.

Chapter 17

MANAGING CHALLENGES OF THE INITIAL GRIEF PERIOD

U NFORTUNATELY THE DEATH OF A LOVED ONE IS NOT UNKNOWN to me. And I realize this is true for many people. No one is immune to losing people they love at some point in time. I lost all my grandparents before I was twelve years old. Then, when I was thirty-five, I lost my dad, who had been my greatest source of encouragement. I lost my mom three years later. In my mid-forties, I lost my friend Kelly Hendren, who was another confidant and source of encouragement. He was a minister who had become a close friend when I was in graduate school. We stayed in touch over the next twenty years with frequent calls and visits. He came to Austin to perform my wedding to Ron and was a part of many family events thereafter. It was a shock when he passed away in his sleep one night due to a heart attack. I've lost several other very close friends since that time as well. It always reminds me that life is short, and we must make the most of every day that we are given. But of course, I am not alone, as we've all lost loved ones and fought through the grief in different ways.

The first few weeks following Ron's death included denial and shock. The denial stage doesn't really mean that we are denying that they have passed away. We know that reality all too well. It's more of waking up or walking into a room where he used to be and thinking, *I can't believe he's not right there!* Or looking at the chair in the living room when you come downstairs and realizing that he's not going to be sitting there anymore. Or walking through the grocery store and realizing you're no longer buying things he asked you to get for him. Some days, even though you know and relive every detail, you're thinking to yourself, *What the heck just happened?*

Life is short, and we must make the most of every day that we are given.

For the first thirty-to-sixty days after losing Ron, I seemed to have the same recurring nightmare. I would wake up feeling anger, frustration, and guilt all over again. In my dreams, I was in his MD Anderson hospital room, and he was declining with more adverse effects of the meds, not getting the needed hydration to prevent kidney failure, not getting the thickened liquids recommended by the swallow study, or not getting the help he needed for whatever his latest symptom might be, and I felt helpless to fix the problem. In this nightmare, everything seemed to be my fault, and I couldn't get to the needed people to help Ron. I would finally wake up and try to tell myself that everyone did everything possible to help him. But then the next night I would have the same nightmare, resulting in some degree of morning trauma and guilt. If only I could have been on the telehealth call where they prescribed the antipsychotic for his anxiety that led to decreased swallowing coordination, which led to the PEG tube and no nutrition/hydration for three days while they waited to complete the procedure, then to X-ray the results, then to finally connect it. Or why didn't I fight to get a higher cc (cubic centimeter) level of hydration in his IV while waiting so long for the NG tube? Or why didn't I beg him even more to get the PEG tube during radiation to prevent his decline in function, affecting his immunity/malnutrition and leading to the onset of acute leukemia?

I know he adamantly refused the PEG tube and promised he would try to drink more protein drinks, but they were too painful. Why didn't I convince him to just try the PEG tube for a few weeks while his throat recovered?

For several months after his death, I experienced many calls, long hold times, and eventual conversations with different accounts and customer service reps regarding paying bills, closing accounts, getting access to accounts, and getting accounts changed to my name so I was allowed communication with them. This was unexpected and overwhelming for several weeks. And just when I thought I had spoken with every person on every account possible, another bill would come in the mail. Over and over again, I would finally get to a live person who would tell me some amount was owed, but then they would usually tell me they are not authorized to speak with me, and they would have to speak with Ronald Milliken himself. Sometimes this would be after thirty-to-sixty minutes on hold and being transferred to different people, and I would have to retell the same story of him passing away. Then I would get the new person who is supposed to know the story by now, and they would tell me the same thing. I think I'm normally a patient person who realizes the individual on the phone is just the messenger doing their job and saying what they have been told to say. But after having these same conversations many times a week with different people and being on hold for what seemed to be the entire morning, with growing anxiety I admit that some days I just lost my patience and started telling the poor person that no one is listening to me! That Ron cannot come to the phone because he's no longer here!

For example, in March 2023, I called our insurance lady from the hospital while by Ron's side in the dialysis unit and then by his side in the ICU. Ron usually dealt with this, but I got her number from his phone and called to discuss a homeowner's potential claim. I also gave her my phone number and email address and asked her to please contact me directly, as Ron couldn't talk and I would be paying all the bills. Of course, at that point I thought he would eventually recover, but I was planning to manage all the finances until he was better. She was very kind and promised she would keep my number and contact me directly if anything was needed.

She did call back to tell me the homeowner's policy would not cover my recent $6,000 plumbing bill to replace all the faulty gas pipes. But I never heard from her again. I called her in June, about a month after Ron's passing, to tell her I wanted to sell Ron's car but was waiting for the probate to get the title in my name. I asked about paying the insurance, and she said to wait until I sold the car, then update my account to put it all in my name. She assured me everything was fine until then. Then in July, after Ron's passing, I somehow recalled that we usually paid our auto insurance in late June and late December, so I called her again. She responded that it was due two weeks ago and that an email had gone to Ron's email address telling him it was time to make the payment. This was very frustrating, but she said, "Oh, that's all automated, so you'll have to log on and change the account to your name and add your email address." I reminded her that she had told me not to change anything to my name yet and that I had given her my contact information, but she seemed oblivious to that information. After changing everything to my name and setting up all the correct account information, I received a follow-up email that still said it was the Ronald Milliken policy. For some reason that triggered tears that lasted for several hours.

That sounds so crazy now, but it stemmed from months of trying to get everything under control and everyone only wanting to speak with him and keep everything in his name. And no matter how many hours I spent initiating the needed phone conversations, it seemed to never end. I had sent death certificates to everyone possible, completed all the necessary new forms, spoken with as many people as possible, and had spent hours of my time on hold, trying to get to a live person. In many cases there was a thirty-to-sixty-day wait period before the needed accounts were resolved and in my name. A similar thing happened with my mobile phone carrier, my cable internet provider, and then a physician's office where they had billed the wrong insurance one year prior, so it was now too late to rebill, and I needed to pay the full amount.

I'm only sharing these frustrations because I know there are so many others who endure the death of a loved one who previously managed their finances, and therefore they experience such challenges.

I now understand what those families are probably going through. It adds a significantly higher level of stress to the grief process for several months after losing someone.

The life insurance company added even more stress, which was completely unexpected. Eighteen months before Ron's passing, his ten-year life insurance policy was up for renewal, so they increased his monthly payments to a much higher rate. So he cancelled the policy, as he also had a smaller policy with his company. Then, two weeks after cancelling, he decided to reinstate his secondary policy but at a lower policy amount, which would take him back to a reasonable monthly cost. That was all before he received his first diagnosis—when he was doing well and had just received a perfect physician's report from his annual physical. When he passed, they treated his policy as a new policy, as it was less than two years old. That means they must question everything from wrongful death to fraud.

The agent in charge of such investigations contacted me and required me to send a ten-year summary of every physician he had seen, along with their respective contact information. Then I had to go through all the records and develop a running spreadsheet of every doctor's office visit and reason for each visit for the past ten years. Thankfully he had been very healthy, but I had to include every dermatology visit, dental office visit, carpal tunnel surgery eight years ago, cardiology visit to check his cholesterol levels, etc. That took several days. When I thought I had finally submitted everything that they had requested, I had to schedule time for a call with them for what I later realized was an interrogation. This ended up being a two-hour call where I had to relive every detail of his diagnosis, symptoms, hospitalizations, medical decisions, responses to treatments, and everything related to those factors. I felt that she somehow wanted to blame me for his death! It was the most traumatizing phone call of all. I cried throughout my accounts of each step along his journey in his attempts to get the needed treatments and eventually how they had all failed.

Again, I now understand all too well what other people must endure during this horrible experience! People going through grief should not have to deal with this. Hopefully most people have a life insurance policy that is more than two years old; otherwise, I have a whole new respect for what the grieving family member may be experiencing.

Throughout Ron's illness, and for the three years following the deletion of my corporate position due to COVID, I had been working as an independent contractor. This meant I was always seeing clients at a clinic and for a home health company while developing new courses for three different companies as well as for a few independent organizations and teaching them online or in person. My son and I were on Ron's insurance. His salary also paid most of the bills, as my income would be sporadic, depending on each of my individual contracts. For instance, I may work several hours each week to research and develop one big course, to then go through pre-production edits, but would not be paid for that course until it was finally filmed. Having an LLC and working as an independent contractor had many rewards, but when Ron's illness and poor prognosis became a reality, I felt a huge need for more stability. I needed a regular monthly salary with the benefits of health insurance and a 401(k). Otherwise, my amygdala felt as if it was taking over my brain with fears of financial instability. Throughout his illness and subsequent death, I felt overwhelmed by this added lack of financial security.

Other triggers of increased stress were surprising. For instance, every time I tried to go to church, which would normally be a source of peace and refuge, I would experience comments from well-meaning people that triggered tears and new levels of distress. The worst and most dreaded statement was, "How are you doing?"—with a big stress on the accented "*do*ing." Now if this came from my closest friends, I would accept it as the fact that they really care because they had been with me throughout the process and did everything possible to offer support. But when it comes from someone who would otherwise never speak to me, although it is probably well-meaning, it feels like an invasion of privacy. I am *not* going to allow myself to break down in public to a person I barely know.

Another surprising and contradicting source of stress was Christian music, where the artist is singing about their sadness with lines such as, "I could hardly breathe," or, "life is unfair," or, "barely surviving." While these songs may be powerful, and some people may relate deeply to those feelings, I can't listen to them. When I listen to music, I want to be encouraged and feel joy! I do not want to have my sadness validated, as that might instead just serve to maintain the deep level of grief and cause me to spiral further downward. I want to be positive and optimistic, as that is my nature. Living for long periods in sadness is the opposite of what I would ever want! Instead, I would channel surf on my Sirius radio until I found a song of hope and joy. It may be from several different Christian radio stations, or from the seventies or eighties channel, or maybe from an upbeat instrumental channel.

> **When I listen to music, I want to be encouraged and feel joy! I do not want to have my sadness validated, as that might instead just serve to maintain the deep level of grief and cause me to spiral further downward.**

The early grief process included denial and shock, nightmares, endless calls to get the needed accounts paid and in my name, life insurance trauma, and fear of financial instability. But several months later, after all the steps to work through each one, things started to settle down. Life moved forward to a new and different level of normal.

Resilience during the early months of grief included a lot of physical exercise to channel my stress. Then I focused on little daily victories, such as getting enough sleep and hydration and checking in with a few close friends. I was beyond blessed to get a great full-time position with a phenomenal group of people. This allowed me to put all my thoughts into working long days on several big projects. To clarify, working a long day is not a bad thing for me. I am energized by achieving goals. I feel the positive adrenaline release by checking off my big to-do lists. So the opportunity to be assigned such big tasks became a blessing. Then I would compartmentalize my grief to Sundays, where I would sometimes need to cry for several hours but would get it out of my system and feel re-energized by Monday morning to start the day with a long jog, then be back at my desk, ready to take on the world by 8 a.m.

The next level of resilience came from eventually being able to say certain things out loud to a few of my closest friends in our one-on-one conversations. Once you speak certain things, ranging from guilt to fear to current struggles, it helps to put things into perspective and stop fearing worst-case scenarios. You are better able to tame your own amygdala and emotions. Prayer is another way to achieve this. Saying audible prayers allows me to focus on how I am grateful for the protection and direction from God. He brings hope as He is much greater than me, and I trust Him to bring me new life and new joy.

One of my long-term positive habits occurs when I first start out on my way to a destination in the car. I begin to pray out loud, telling God all the things for which I am grateful! The more I focus on this list, the less important the list of stresses and fears seems to be. Then I realize the importance of focusing on my blessings rather than fearing the unknown, or things over which I have no control. It becomes obvious to me that dwelling on negative circumstances is counterproductive.

Celebrate each small victory every day. This may include more hydration today than yesterday, a longer walk this morning, or a task completed at work. Speak the words out loud of what you are grateful for, which might start with a place to live, a car to drive, friends and family, etc. Then, keep adding to that list. This shifts your brain to a better place and allows resiliency and strength.

Chapter 18

RESILIENT STEPS, MOVING FORWARD

THE WORLD HEALTH ORGANIZATION DEFINES HEALTH AS "A state of complete physical, mental, and social well-being and not merely the absence of disease or infirmity (illness)."[30] Though this definition originated in 1948, it is still a revelation to realize that we are not considered to be well only when we do not have a disease. To really be well, we must include the physical, mental, and social levels of well-being. The goal of resilience is to achieve wellness in all of these levels when recovering from adversity and rising above the challenges of life with a higher level of strength than before.

This final chapter will focus on direct actions and strategies we can add to our daily lives to achieve the highest levels of resilience over each of our unique challenges and to attain a higher quality of life. I'll share these well-researched recommendations in a list format for ease of later reference. I incorporate many of these in my own

---

30. "WHO Remains Firmly Committed to the Principles Set Out in the Preamble to the Constitution," World Health Organization, 2024, https://www.who.int/about/accountability/governance/constitution.

life. The individuals who have shared their stories report to have used some of these strategies as well in their own pursuit of wellness.

- *Practice self-care:* The basic foundation of our wellness starts with eating right, hydrating, sleeping, and practicing relaxation. Many of us do not like to focus on ourselves when others need our attention, and we need to spend all our efforts elsewhere. But the fact is that if we do not schedule time to care for these basic needs, we will continue to rapidly decline in our own health. Scheduling periodic health maintenance, including dental and eye examinations, is also essential to this foundation of caring for ourselves.

- *Optimize nutrition:* A healthy diet can help counter the impact of stress by shoring up the immune system and lowering blood pressure. Some foods can cut levels of cortisol and adrenaline, which are those stress hormones that take a toll on the body over time. Comfort foods, like a bowl of warm oatmeal, boost levels of serotonin, which is a calming brain chemical. Other foods that have been cited as stress busters include complex carbs, oranges, spinach, fatty fish, black tea, pistachios, avocados, almonds, raw veggies, and milk.

- *Hydrate:* A study from the University of Connecticut showed that even mild dehydration can cause mood problems. By the time you feel thirsty, it's too late. We may not even feel thirst until we are one or two percent dehydrated. Since our brain mass is 75 percent water, research has related our ability to think and to respond with optimal cognitive abilities to our levels of hydration.[31]

- *Keep moving:* Physical activity can help lower overall stress levels and improve quality of life both mentally and physically. Exercising regularly can relieve the tension, anxiety, anger, and mild depression that often goes hand in

31. Na Zhang, Song M. Du, Jian F. Zhang, and Guan S. Ma, "Effects of Dehydration and Rehydration on Cognitive Performance and Mood among Male College Students in Cangzhou, China: A Self-Controlled Trial," *International Journal of Environmental Research and Public Health* 16, no. 11 (May 29, 2019): 1,891, https://doi.org/10.3390/ijerph16111891.

hand with stress. It can improve the quality of sleep, which can be negatively impacted by stress, depression, and anxiety. Chapter three of this book provides many details,

Exercising regularly can relieve the tension, anxiety, anger, and mild depression that often goes hand in hand with stress.

including specific research on the benefits of exercise in these references on physical resilience.

- *Get quality sleep:* Anxiety causes sleeping problems, and sleep deprivation can cause anxiety disorders—so it becomes a vicious cycle of the increased effects of stress from a lack of quality sleep patterns. A few tips for improving sleep include moving your body earlier in the day; creating the right sleep environment (e.g., controlling light, sound, and temperature); limiting caffeine and alcohol, especially in evening hours; hydrating until 6 p.m.; calming your mind by utilizing relaxation techniques throughout the day; and limiting television, phone, and tablet screen time by turning them off one hour before bedtime, listening to music or reading a book instead. If needed, ask for help from your doctor or a counselor. Improving sleep can make a dramatic difference in obtaining resilience.

- *Schedule time for things that bring joy:* This could include your hobbies of interest (e.g., painting, hiking, sewing, building a birdhouse, reading), spending time with a friend (e.g., taking a Zumba class, taking a pottery class, playing golf, meeting for coffee), or going to a new place of interest (e.g., to a new restaurant, the beach, a sporting event, a museum).

- *Commit to a wellness partner:* This could include engagement in goal-oriented discussions that lead to emotional wellness, spiritual wellness, physical wellness, and social wellness.

- *Realize the benefits of daily journaling:* Journaling can allow us to clarify our thoughts and feelings and to gain valuable self-knowledge. It also decreases the symptoms of asthma, arthritis, and other health conditions, improves cognitive functioning, strengthens immune system response, and counteracts many of the negative effects of stress. Journaling is a wonderful way to build personal resilience. The following are three types of journaling one can practice in an effort reach their goals:

>> *Gratitude journal:* Every day, list three things for which you are grateful. This helps to focus on current resources, create a positive mood, and build resilience.

>> *Emotional release:* Write your emotional responses to events each day. This helps process what we're feeling and explore more positive reframing options.

>> *Bullet journal/personal planning journal:* Track what you need to do each day. Include goals, memories created, etc. This helps to keep our minds uncluttered and to remember what's important. Being more organized and balanced is a great way to feel less stressed.[32]

• *Prioritize social connections and relationships:* Quality relationships are important for our well-being, but there's significant research that shows how stress affects our personal relationships. To address and reduce the amount of stress that affects our connectedness with others, seek first the source of stress, such as an overwhelming job, a personal crisis, an illness, etc. Set boundaries with friends/family members (e.g., number of minutes and when to talk about the source of stress each day), then practice self-care with your spouse or confide in other close relationships. Utilize other strategies such as journaling to put your challenges into perspective, which will prevent a shift of blame or other negative reactions to your loved one. Good social connections add to our quality of life, but loneliness and isolation has been frequently connected to the formation of disease and decreased immunity. On a

32. Joshua M. Smyth, Jillian A. Johnson, Brandon J. Auer, Erik Lehman, Giampaolo Talamo, and Christopher N. Sciamanna, "Online Positive Affect Journaling in the Improvement of Mental Distress and Well-Being in General Medical Patients with Elevated Anxiety Symptoms: A Preliminary Randomized Controlled Trial," *JMIR Mental Health* 5, no. 4 (June 13, 2018), doi:10.2196/11290.

related note, remove negative relationships from your life that can drain your energy and add further stress and anxiety, which is counterproductive to resilience.

- *Set boundaries to achieve a work-life balance:* (Note: this is the hardest one for me to achieve, but I'm constantly trying to achieve it despite my failures in the past in this area.) Dr. Dike Drummond advises us to focus on the following sequential points:

  » *Step one:* Put *you* first. Life balance can only happen when you say "yes" to priorities outside of work or other time-consuming tasks. Reflect on what you want in your life outside of your current overwhelming schedule. Make a list of the things that are really important to you.

  » *Step two:* Put your priorities on your calendar. Write your non-work priorities on your calendar (in ink) for several months ahead. For example, events with family, exercise, dinner with a friend, weekend activities, or vacation. Then, when important non-work activities are already on your calendar, you can say "no" to build work-life balance with some grace.

  » *Step three:* Say "no" with power and skill. Now you have said "yes" to your life with boundaries, so you use "no" to defend your already existing calendar of higher priorities. When your work-life balance is challenged, you can say, "I'm so sorry, I have another very important activity already scheduled at that exact time."

- *Add music to your day:* Music can be a powerful stress management tool. Music activates a widespread bilateral network of brain regions (frontal, temporal, parietal, and subcortical) related to attention, working memory, semantic and syntactic processing, motor functions, and emotional processing.[33] Listening to music has significant effects on

---

33. Dana L. Strait, Nina Kraus, Erika Skoe, and Richard Ashley, "Musical Experience and Neural Efficiency: Effects of Training on Subcortical Processing of Vocal Expressions of Emotion," *The European Journal of Neuroscience* 29, no. 3 (February 2, 2009): 661–668, https://doi.org/10.1111/j.1460-9568.2009.06617.x.

psychobiological stress in an everyday life setting. Listening to music (especially for relaxation) in the presence of others increases this stress-reducing effect. At the same time, listening to music in daily life differentially affects the HPA (hypothalamic-pituitary-adrenal) axis and autonomic nervous system functioning.[34]

- *Practice relaxation techniques:* Direct actions to practice physical and mental relaxation actually trigger a process that lessens the stress effects on the mind and body. The Mayo Clinic sites the physiological effects of relaxation techniques, which include a slower heart rate, lower blood pressure, slower breathing rate, improved digestion, controlled blood sugar levels, decreased release of stress hormones, increased blood flow to major muscles, eased muscle tension and chronic pain, improved focus and mood, improved sleep quality, lower fatigue, decreased anger and frustration, and increased confidence to handle challenges. Examples of the techniques include visualization, meditation, tai chi or yoga, breathing exercises, and progressive muscle relaxation.[35]

- *Try box breathing:* This is an example of a simple breathing/relaxation technique that makes a big difference in decreasing stress and increasing focus. Here are the easy steps: breathe in for a count of five, hold for a count of five, then slowly breathe out for a count of five. Pause for a count of five, then repeat the process.

- *Practice mindful meditation:* Meditation serves dual roles of reducing stress and restoring energy. Mindful breathing is a quick technique for relaxing and re-centering yourself. Take a few moments during the day to sit comfortably in a chair, close your eyes, and pay attention to your breathing and the

34. Alexandra Linnemann, Jana Strahler, and Urs M. Nater, "Assessing the Effects of Music Listening on Psychobiological Stress in Daily Life," *Journal of Visualized Experiments* 120 (February 2, 2017): DOI: 10.3791/54920.

35. "Relaxation Techniques: Try These Steps to Lower Stress," Mayo Clinic, Mayo Foundation for Medical Education and Research, January 24, 2024, https://www.mayoclinic.org/healthy-lifestyle/stress-management/in-depth/relaxation-technique/art-20045368.

sensations it creates. Take a series of slow or deep breaths, feeling the release and relaxation of the cleansing out-breath.

- *Pray:* Prayer and spiritual practice reduce stress and anxiety. Just twelve minutes of prayer per day may actually slow down the aging process. Contemplating a loving God rather than a punitive god reduces anxiety, depression, and stress, and increases feelings of security, compassion, and love. Intense prayer and meditation permanently change numerous structures and functions in the brain.[36] Prayer also includes focusing our attention on those things for which we are thankful. It includes worshiping our Creator, which shifts our perspective from our own situation and allows us to then trust God for a new resolve. Worship is a declaration that God is with us, and He will support us through all that is happening in our own adversity. He is a powerful weapon against any challenge or obstacle. Worshiping with other people is a type of social resilience, which helps us to submit and surrender all our cares and worries to God—this includes our priorities, plans, hopes, dreams, and even our fears. Prayer and meditation both work to tame the amygdala, which is the hub of fear memory, and actually increase the gray matter density of the brain.[37]

Worship is a declaration that God is with us, and He will support us through all that is happening in our own adversity. He is a powerful weapon against any challenge or obstacle.

- *Laugh!* Laughter is a powerful tool that reduces the stress hormones known to suppress immunity. It also activates T cells,

36. Andrew B. Newberg and Mark Robert Waldman, *How God Changes Your Brain: Breakthrough Findings from a Leading Neuroscientist* (NY: Ballantine Books, 2010).

37. Eileen Luders, Arthur W. Toga, Natasha Lepore, and Christian Gaser, "The Underlying Anatomical Correlates of Long-Term Meditation: Larger Hippocampal and Frontal Volumes of Gray Matter," *Neuroimage* 45, no. 3 (April 15, 2009): 672–678, doi: 10.1016/j.neuroimage.2008.12.061.

immunoglobulins, and natural killer cells, which collectively play a role in rejecting tumors and cells infected with viruses and protecting us from infection. It increases beta-endorphins, which improve mood, reduce pain, and increase relaxation.[38]

- *Seek benefits from volunteering:* When we leave our normal responsibilities, challenges, and work world to volunteer, it has been found to shift our focus from our own world to that of helping others. And in the process, this shift of mental focus has been found to result in physical and mental benefits, such as lower mortality rates, greater functional ability, lower rates of depression, increased physical and social activity, and a greater sense of purpose. Volunteerism may also improve memory and the ability to provide help and support to peers.

- *Kill the ANTs—automatic negative thoughts:* Killing the ANTs is a very effective cognitive behavioral therapy. For example, replace the ANT "I'll never be able to _____ again" with "I'm going to try something new, and I'm looking forward to it!" Our brains get infested by daily negative thoughts that rob our joy and steal our happiness. Every time we have a thought, our brain releases chemicals to make the body feel the way we think and vice versa. For this reason, it is very important to be aware of what we are thinking.

- *Decrease social media time:* People often post their best moments and photos online. The same people may be going through tremendous challenges or depression and anxiety that they do not share. But the rest of us see all the beautiful people, with what appears to be their perfect children, who are all living their perfect life. And then when we see those posts, we may find ourselves feeling left out and feeling less about their own life. The truth is that no one has the perfect

38. R. I. M. Dunbar, Rebecca Baron, Anna Frangou, Eiluned Pearce, Edwin J. C. van Leeuwen, Julie Stow, Giselle Partridge, Ian MacDonald, Vincent Barra, and Mark van Vugt, "Social Laughter Is Correlated with an Elevated Pain Threshold," *Proceedings of the Royal Society: Biological Sciences* 279, 1731 (September 14, 2011): 1,161–1,167, https://doi.org/10.1098/rspb.2011.1373.

life. We should not dwell on how others have more than what we have. We are all in this life together doing the best we can. When we decrease time on social media, we stop such unhealthy thoughts and comparisons of ourselves to others.

These stress management techniques are some of the most effective, natural, and evidence-based methods to build the resilience levels that are needed for us to achieve a higher quality of life. Each of us will find different strategies to be most helpful as we seek our own way. We all have different abilities and respond better to some than others. But I pray that each of you finds the things that work for you, because not seeking the steps you need will result in a lesser quality of life than you deserve.

Even if you can't exercise an hour a day due to physical limitations, or if you can't spend the weekend volunteering, or if your time is limited, there is still something here for all of us that will lead us to rise above whatever challenges may come our way. Everyone has the ability to work through their own steps to resiliency, and everyone deserves the highest quality of life.

As you read through the list of strategies that promote wellness and subsequently build resilience, pick two or three of these things to start applying to your life every day. Write them down, and make an effort to check each off your list every day. Small, daily changes can result in a major increase to your quality of life.

APPENDIX I:
Prisoner in a Beautiful Small Room

BY PATTY MOWER PANNI[39]

she chooses artwork that she loves
decorates the mantle just so
hangs a pretty wreath on the inside of the door
she shifts the lighting, from a.m. bright to p.m. dim
her design theme is cozy coastal
because she loves blues and greens
the shades of sea and land, but
a prisoner surrounded by beautiful things is still a prisoner
outside, nature displays its grand artwork
in leaves that turn, curl, droop, drop
greens to brilliant oranges, reds, yellows, browns
skies cobalt to amber, pink, and purple, fade to black
as a child, she ran, jumped, crawled
roller-skated and danced in pure jubilation
her body belonged to itself, had not yet betrayed itself
the prisoner had not yet been condemned
not many years past she walked in the early morning cool

39. Poem used with permission.

PRISONER IN A BEAUTIFUL SMALL ROOM

every day without fail, lacing up her shoes to greet the dawn
if she'd known that the last time would be the last time
she might've never gone home
so now she sits surrounded by beautiful things
but yearns only for what she'll never have again

APPENDIX II:
Example Scenarios of First Steps to Resiliency

B ELOW ARE A FEW STEPS TO START THE PROCESS TOWARD resiliency. Everyone could begin their day with prayer or meditation and gratefulness. Then, just add two-to-three things into your day to start making a big difference in your level of resiliency.

1. If you work a lot and feel stress but do not have a lot of time,

   » Find an exercise buddy, and commit to meeting them for an exercise class, walk, or gym visit three times/week. You'll be surprised what is possible to fit in this thirty-to-sixty-minute plan three times/week, and it will make a huge difference in how you think and feel.

   » At work, take a ten-minute break every two-to-three hours to eat a snack of protein or fruit with twelve-to-sixteen ounces of water. Then take a brief walk around the workplace or walk up/down the stairs. You'll be more productive for the rest of the day and will feel more energy.

   » Practice box breathing for five minutes when you feel high levels of stress during your day. This lowers stress hormones, relaxes your body, and calms your mind.

2. If you have health difficulties that limit your ability to exercise,

   » Find an easy class, or online video, or adaptive yoga class to do. The breathing and stretching techniques increase blood flow; warms up muscles; eases pain; alleviates discomfort in tender, swollen joints; and most importantly decreases stress hormones.

   » Volunteer for an organization or community project to help others. This challenges your brain, decreases stress and depression, increases socialization, and adds light physical activity.

» Journal a few thoughts each day to focus on how you are helping others and what you can do while committing to stop any thoughts about what you cannot do.

3. If you have health difficulties that *prevent* your ability to exercise,

» First, develop a plan for enough sleep, the right nutrition (protein, fruits, and vegetables), and hydration.

» Plan time to go outside every day when possible or to spend time with a friend. Seek sources of laughter every day!

» Spend ten minutes each day stretching and/or working on a deep breathing or box breathing exercise.

» Journal thoughts, including what you are grateful for or other positive thoughts, to replace the automatic negative thoughts (ANTs).

4. If you are a caregiver who cares for a loved one full time,

» First, assess your own health. This should include a regular doctor's visit for lab work and a plan for maintaining your own health. If you neglect your own health, you will not be able to care for someone else.

» Find sources of laughter to release stress and physical tension.

» Seek help from others to give you a break in your day, even if it is thirty minutes, to go for a walk, take a nap, attend an exercise class, or do something you enjoy. Your brain and body will be able to regroup and function better for the day following this moment of respite.

» Practice box breathing throughout the day at any point when you feel escalating stress.

5. If you are pulled in many directions to care for others (e.g., children, parents, neighbors) and are responsible for many tasks (e.g., work, volunteer jobs, household responsibilities),

» Add to your giant to-do list something that includes your own self-care, at least two-to-three times/week (e.g., your own exercise, time to laugh with a friend).
» Keep a running journal entry of your sleep, hydration, and nutrition schedule. Look for any patterns of depletion, and seek to directly address those. This could make a big difference in your energy and strength to get to everything on your to-do list.
» Delegate tasks where possible, and say "no" to new requests of others if at all possible.

Practice box breathing for five minutes every day to decrease stress, relax your body, and calm your mind.

www.ingramcontent.com/pod-product-compliance
Lightning Source LLC
Chambersburg PA
CBHW052046090426
42739CB00010B/2061